Principal Events in

	National and International	*Regional*
January	Japanese evacuation of Guadalcanal begins. Casablanca Conference of Churchill, Roosevelt and Chiefs of Staff. Siege of Leningrad raised. Montgomery and 8th Army make triumphal entry into Tripoli. USAAF first bombing raid on Germany—Wilhelmshaven. RAF daylight raid on Berlin. Paulas surrender ends German offensive in Russia.	First Anglo-American weddings in East Anglia. First USAAF raid on German targets. RAF Mosquitoes from Marham make first raid on Berlin.
February	Mopping-up in Stalingrad. Churchill visits Tripoli. Russians capture Kursk, Rostov and Karkov. RAF and USAAF step up bombing raids on German industrial targets and Atlantic bases.	Cambridgeshire men in action in Tunisia. All East Anglian towns join Cambridge celebration of 25th anniversary of Red Army. Government majority reduced in King's Lynn by-election.
March	Spring thaw immobilises armies on Russian front. Darwin raided by Japanese aircraft. Worst period for Allied shipping losses in Battle of Atlantic.	Essex Regiment in heavy fighting in Tunisia. 13 WRNS killed in raid on Great Yarmouth. First list of Japanese POWs received.
April	End of U-boat dominance of Atlantic. British and US forces link in Tunisia. Germans destroy Warsaw ghetto. Eighth Army captures Sfax, Sousse and Enfidaville in Tunisia.	Coastal belt designated "regulated area". Heavy raid on Chelmsford—prison and county offices damaged. Norfolk-born candidate wins first Commons seat for new Common Wealth party.
May	Tunis captured. US troops take Bizerta on same day. All German and Italian troops in North Africa surrender. African continent clear of Axis forces. RAF bomb dams and flood Ruhr valley.	Bishop's Palace at Norwich becomes American Red Cross Forces Club. Essex and Cambridgeshire troops take part in capture of Tunis. Luftwaffe starts low-level raids on East Anglian ports with fighter-bombers—many killed.

EAST ANGLIA 1943

by

R. DOUGLAS BROWN

TERENCE DALTON LIMITED
LAVENHAM . SUFFOLK
1990

Published by
TERENCE DALTON LIMITED

ISBN 0 86138 074 6

Text photoset in 10/12pt Times

Printed in Great Britain at
The Lavenham Press Limited, Lavenham, Suffolk

Contents

Publishers' Note

The publishers regret that the reproduction of certain illustrations is below the quality that they would normally demand. The *East Anglian Daily Times* and the *Eastern Daily Press*, who kindly permitted us the use of their files, were unfortunately unable to provide original photographs and, consequently, the pictures shown are reproductions from the printed newspapers. The same applies to those photographs from the *Cambridge Evening News* that were so kindly provided by the Cambridge Collection of the Cambridgeshire Libraries. Where applicable, it was considered preferable to show illustrations, even if below our usual standard, rather than no pictures at all. This volume is the fifth of a series which will fully document the events in East Anglia, year by year, and we would welcome any photographs that apply to 1944 or subsequent years. These would be forwarded to the author for his use and duly returned.

To Ann
who arrived in 1943

Index of Illustrations

Introduction and Acknowledgements

THE STORY of East Anglia in 1943 is unique in the whole history of the region. The events in which its people were involved did not all take place within the eastern counties. Many thousands of men were serving in the armed forces far from home; some fighting in Italy or sailing with the Royal Navy, some training in different parts of the British Isles or in India for great battles that were later to determine the outcome of the war, some held as prisoners-of-war in enemy territory. Many of the latter were suffering great hardship and privation as Japanese slave labour on the construction of a new railway to link Siam and Burma.

Another part of the story of East Anglia in 1943 concerns tens of thousands of men who ate and slept and relaxed in the region, but who went forth week by week to fight their way in the skies over Germany and the occupied territories of Europe. No area of comparable size has ever been so densely packed with air bases. The life of those bases, though little was known about it by East Anglians at the time, is a fascinating part of the region's history.

On the home front, the situation in 1943 was peculiarly difficult. The majority of husbands and fathers had been conscripted into the Services and were rarely seen. Wives kept the homes running in the face of severe rationing, not only of food but of clothing, fuel, furnishings and most other goods, and did full-time jobs as well—unless they were mothers of young children, in which case their single-parent responsibilities rested heavily upon them. The shortages, the loneliness and the boredom created serious stresses in society.

This was the East Anglia that was almost overwhelmed in 1943 by American airmen and, in the later months, by British troops preparing for the coming invasion of Europe. It was a situation fraught with possibilities of social disaster. Serious problems did arise, and they caused much concern to the authorities, but the great majority of East Anglian homes came through those testing times with flying colours.

Many people recognised the stirring times in which they were living and recorded their experiences and emotions, and I have—as in previous volumes in this series—quoted from those contemporary documents wherever possible. These include a number of personal diaries now held in the Mass Observation Archive at Sussex University, and I wish to express my thanks to the custodians of the Archive for permission to quote from these and from various reports compiled by Mass

Observation during 1943, and to Ms Dorothy Sheridan, BA, the archivist, for her guidance and assistance.

Several remarkable narratives by Americans who served in East Anglia have now been published, and I wish to express my special gratitude to authors and publishers who have given permission for me to quote from *Here We Are Together*, by Robert Arbib; *The Mighty Men of the 381st: Heroes All*, by the Reverend James Good Brown; and *Combat Crew*, by John Comer. These books give a wonderfully detailed account of the Americans' experience among us.

I acknowledge equally my indebtedness to several authoritative histories and their authors: *The History of the Royal Norfolk Regiment*, by Lieutenant-Commander P. K. Kemp; *The Essex Regiment*, by Colonel T. A. Martin; and *The Suffolk Regiment*, by Colonel W. N. Nicholson, and I thank authors and publishers for permission to quote from them. I have also quoted from the following, and wish to express my thanks for permission to do so: *Night Action*, by Captain Peter Dickens; *The GIs—the Americans in Britain, 1942–45*, by Norman Longmate; *When Jim Crow Met John Bull*, by Graham Smith; and *The Burma–Siam Railway*, by Robert Hardie.

I wish also to thank Mr Roger Freeman, whose authoritative histories of the Eighth USAAF have been of great value to me, for his kindness in reading the first two chapters and offering suggestions, and Mr Ian Hawkins, for his assistance with illustrations.

The daily newspapers published during 1943 in Norwich, Ipswich and Cambridge have been a principal source for events on the home front, and I wish to thank the Eastern Counties Newspapers Group Ltd and Cambridge Newspapers Ltd, and the editors of the various newspapers, for permission to quote from their reports and to reprint some of their photographs.

I have made use of primary sources where possible and I wish to express appreciation of the co-operation of staff at the Public Record Office at Kew, the Departments of Books and Photographs at the Imperial War Museum, the Local Studies Department of the Norfolk County Library at Norwich, the Cambridgeshire Local History Collection at Cambridge Central Library, and the Suffolk Record Office at Bury St Edmunds and Ipswich.

For the national and international background of the period I have depended upon the various volumes of the official war history published by Her Majesty's Stationery Office, and Sir Winston Churchill's personal account, *The Second World War*.

R. DOUGLAS BROWN

Stoke-by-Clare, Suffolk.
July, 1989.

CHAPTER ONE

Forging a Striking Force

THE ENGLAND of 1943 has been likened to an aircraft carrier anchored just off the coast of an enemy-occupied continent. East Anglia, then, was the flight deck. Here a thousand or more planes flew, day and night, from over one hundred airfields to attack targets in Europe. There was no hour when the sky did not seem full of aircraft; often there were dozens, and occasionally even hundreds, to be seen at the same time. On a sunny summer morning they sometimes glittered like enormous chandeliers hanging in the sky as they took up formation and flew off to the east. In the dusk of a winter evening they looked like dark predators as they swooped down to their bases. When darkness veiled their presence, the air still throbbed with the noise of countless engines. In a twenty-four-hour cycle there were sometimes as many as four thousand flight movements over the region, and the airfields were so closely spaced across the eastern counties that it was difficult to keep the planes apart and to get them down safely.

The aircraft, the airfields and the airmen dominated the life of the East Anglians. This phenomenon developed from the earliest days of the war, at first slowly as Britain struggled to fill the serious gaps in its defences, then with a steadily increasing momentum as war factories and construction firms got into their stride.

As 1943 began the Royal Air Force was already a substantial presence in the region. No 3 Group of Bomber Command, with its headquarters at Exning, near Newmarket, was operating from a score of airfields, flying Stirlings and Wellingtons. A "Pathfinder" Force had recently been formed, with its headquarters at Wyton in Huntingdonshire, and its planes flew regularly from Wyton, Graveley, Oakington and Warboys to drop indicator bombs on targets in the German heartland. During 1942 Honington and Bassingbourn had despatched Wellington bombers to form part of the first thousand-plane raids on Germany. Other RAF aircraft operated against shipping and airfields in enemy-occupied countries across the Channel, and there were a dozen RAF fighter stations near the east coast.

The build-up of RAF strength brought many strangers into the eastern counties, not only from other parts of Britain but from the far corners of the world. By 1st January, 1943, thirty-seven per cent of Bomber Command pilots were

While mechanics work on one of the Wright Cyclone engines of a B-17 of the 323rd Bombardment Squadron at Bassingbourn another ground crew member paints up yet another "mission completed" symbol. The 323rd was a unit of the 91st Bomb Group, which had arrived at Bassingbourn in October, 1942.

Imperial War Museum

Canadians, Australians or New Zealanders, and airmen from most of the occupied countries of western Europe and from Poland and Czechoslovakia were also serving at East Anglian bases. But the arrivals who literally transformed the life of the region were the Americans.

There is a sense in which it may be said that the American air force "grew up" in East Anglia. At the outbreak of the war—when it was known as the Army Air Corps—its total strength was only 20,000; by the end of 1943 there were 185,000 airmen in England, most of them in the eastern counties. When the United States entered the war, it was planned to send sixty heavy bomb groups to operate B-17 Fortress and B-24 Liberator aircraft from the United Kingdom, plus fifteen groups of medium bombers and twenty-five fighter groups—something like 3,500 aircraft, to be distributed over some seventy-five airfields. In fact, the US Eighth Air Force (the "Mighty Eighth") eventually occupied 122 airfields; its combat groups were all concentrated in an area measuring forty by eighty miles, extending from Northampton eastwards to the sea.

To speed these powerful new Allied forces to Britain's aid, the RAF gave up many of its airfields, and construction of new bases put in hand during 1942 was pressed forward with a new sense of urgency. The first airfields in the eastern counties used by the United States Army Air Force were Grafton Underwood (near Kettering), Chelveston (near Wellingborough), Molesworth (near Huntingdon) and Polebrook (near Oundle), which all had an American presence by July, 1942. As 1943 began the Stars and Stripes also fluttered from the flagpoles of former RAF bases at Alconbury, Bassingbourn, Debden, Duxford, Honington, Horsham St Faiths, Thurleigh and Wattisham.

Bassingbourn was the first American base in Cambridgeshire; the 91st Bomb Group arrived there at mid-October, 1942. The first in Norfolk were at Shipdham, where the 44th Bomb Group arrived in October, and at Hardwick, which received the 93rd Bomb Group in December, both groups flying B-24 Liberators. In Suffolk, the Eighth Air Force's bombers first appeared at Bury St Edmunds (Rougham), Horham and Rattlesden: the 47th Bomb Group, a unit of the Twelfth Air Force, arrived at Bury in September, 1942, with A-20 Havocs, moving on to Horham on 5th October, and the 322nd Bomb Group at Rattlesden in December, with two squadrons of B-26 Marauders. In December personnel of the 322nd Bomb Group took over Rougham, but their Marauders did not follow until late March, 1943.

The airfields from which the USAAF flew fell into three groups. First, there were established RAF airfields from which the British withdrew. Secondly, there were new stations which the government had authorised before America declared war and construction of which began in accordance with Air Ministry standards, but which had then to be upgraded to meet the needs of the USAAF. Thirdly, there were bases which were planned and constructed specifically for the Americans.

The construction programme was the biggest civil engineering programme Britain had ever seen, and every leading contractor was employed: Richard Costain

Ltd, W. & C. French Ltd, John Laing & Son Ltd, Taylor-Woodrow Ltd, George Wimpey & Co. Ltd, and many others. It was given an absolute priority for use of scarce materials, and labour was recruited or conscripted wherever possible: labourers from Ireland, youngsters between their schooldays and Service call-up, women living near the sites. They were paid wages they could only have dreamt of before the war. The Air Ministry estimated the total cost of the new works and expansion required for the joint RAF-USAAF offensive at £615 million.

Some of the airfields which were intended from the outset for the Americans were built by US Army Engineer Battalions, largely composed of black troops. They built Chipping Ongar, Debach, Eye, Glatton, Gosfield, Great Dunmow, Great Saling (Andrews Field), Matching, Nuthampstead and Stansted during 1942–43. Typically, Andrews Field, the first to be completed and officially opened on 21st May, 1943, covered a site two miles square and cost over a million pounds.

B-17F Fortresses of the 96th Bomb Group line up for takeoff at Snetterton Heath, in Norfolk.
USAF

Cambridge Visitors at U.S. Bomber Station

WONDERS OF THE
" FORTS "

Typical American

The visitors, in front of the bomber "Stump Jumper": (Left to right)
Lady Bragg, Mr. John Lowe (Ministry of Information), Ald. E. O. Brown,
Miss Kay Maloney ("Cambridge Daily News" representative), Councillor
Mrs. Hardman, Miss Clapham (M.O.I.), Mr. W. H. Kester, the Mayor
(Ald. W. L. Briggs), Councillor George Wilding, Mrs. De Morpurgo, Miss
Shankland (Director of American Red Cross Club, Bull Hotel) and Mr.
Norman Higgins.

As part of the goodwill effort, USAAF stations in East Anglia invited local representatives to visit the units based in the area. Here visitors from Cambridge pose in front of the B-17F "Stump Jumper". *Cambridge Local Collection*

Working seven days a week, a thousand Americans constructed it in ten months.

The base construction gangs worked night and day in two ten-hour shifts, the machines idle for only two hours after each shift for maintenance. Dinner was taken out to the field in containers to save time. An American who was involved described the scene:

> All day a constant stream of trucks, driven by civilians, and loaded with gravel, sand, cement, rubble from bombed cities, and cinders, rumbled along the narrow lanes and deposited their loads in the stockpiles that rose like small hills on the landscape. Cranes, operated by headquarters company men, loaded our own trucks with these materials . . . The dirtiest of all assignments was that of the cement gang; all day long they stood on their platform, and emptied 100-lb sacks of cement into the trucks that rolled up to them, one a minute . . .[1]

The standard ("Class A") heavy bomber airfield had three intersecting runways, constructed of concrete eight inches thick. The main one was at least 2,000 yards long, the others at least 1,400 yards, and all had a standard width of 50 yards. A perimeter road, 50 feet wide, encircled the flying field, linking the ends of the runways and averaging three miles in length, and off this "peritrack" were hard standings and dispersal points.

There were usually two hangars 240 feet long by 120 feet span by 39 feet high,

4

a control tower with balconies, machine and maintenance shops, Nissen huts to store flying gear and equipment, briefing rooms, and two underground fuel stores holding 100,000 gallons of aviation spirit each. Bomb dumps and ammunition stores were sited well away from the base, with a service road connection, and the accommodation for personnel (in Nissen or similar temporary buildings) was usually at the opposite side of the base, dispersed over ten or more sites, each accommodating two hundred men.

New airfields opened during 1943 and former RAF bases assigned to the Eighth Army Air Force in that year were: in May, Andrews Field, Earls Colne and Framlingham; in June, Boxted, Great Ashfield (near Bury St Edmunds), Knettishall (near Thetford), Snetterton Heath (near Attleborough), Thorpe Abbots (between Diss and Harleston), Ridgewell (from RAF), Great Dunmow and Chipping Ongar; in July, Halesworth, Steeple Morden (from RAF) and Bodney (from RAF); in August, Metfield and Wendling (near East Dereham); in October, East Wretham (near Thetford) and Martlesham Heath (both from RAF); in November, Leiston, Raydon (near Ipswich), Seething (near Norwich), Tibenham and Deenethorpe (east of Corby in Northamptonshire); and in December, Old Buckenham (near Attleborough).

The activity generated by the construction of these bases, and their regular supply when operational, transformed the daily life of much of rural East Anglia. The chief general manager of the London and North Eastern Railway Company, in whose area most of the air bases were situated, spoke of enormous quantities of building materials, petrol and stores of all kinds being carried to the bases, citing a dozen small stations which handled 335,000 tons of goods during the six months ended June, 1943, compared with only 81,000 tons during the six months ended June, 1940.

Whenever RAF airfields were officially handed over to the Americans or construction of a new base by the Americans was completed there was elaborate ceremonial, which provided the country folk in the vicinity with unusual excitement. The Stars and Stripes would be run up in place of the Royal Air Force Ensign and there would be a march-past, with regimental colours held high and a drum and bugle band playing, and with the mobile construction equipment as well as guns and armoured vehicles trundling along behind.

The Germans monitored the progress of these construction projects, and the sites were frequently attacked by the Luftwaffe. At some of them the Americans provided their own anti-aircraft defences while construction was under way; for some time there was a 1,200-strong anti-aircraft regiment based on Rattlesden. In many places, however, the local Home Guard took a large share of the defence duties and usually established happy relations with the Americans.

At Andrews Field and at Debden, for example, the 11th Essex Battalion, Home Guard (Great Dunmow section) worked closely with the Americans, shot side by side with them on improvised ranges, and developed personal off-duty friendships. This relationship gave rise to an odd incident when a German plane was shot down near Andrews Field and its pilot landed by parachute, unhurt, and hurried to give himself up. The first door he knocked on was that of a local public house. The landlord was a Home Guard, and he had just gone to bed after an evening spent with his American friends. Thinking the banging outside was their practical joke, he stuck his head through the window and shouted "go away". The German called in vain at several other private houses before eventually he came to a hospital, where he was recognised and given cocoa while the police were called[2].

To each of its East Anglian airfields the Eighth Army Air Force assigned one bomb group, with an initial complement of thirty-two to thirty-six heavy bombers. Each group consisted of four squadrons, and eventually each squadron had eighteen planes, so that by late 1943 the hard standings at most airfields had to be enlarged to accommodate them.

Eighth Air Force Bomber Command was split into three divisions. The 1st Division established its headquarters at Brampton Grange, in Huntingdonshire; the 2nd Division started with its headquarters at Old Catton, Norwich, then moved

Ground crews surround B-17 "Eight Ball" of the 303rd Bomb Group after its return to Molesworth from a raid on Wilhelmshaven on 27th January. *Imperial War Museum*

to Horsham St Faiths, and in December, 1943, to nearby Ketteringham Hall; and the 3rd was at Elveden Hall, a few miles west of Thetford. Each division was divided into combat wings (of which there were thirteen) and most bomber wings consisted of three groups.

The Americans also had three fighter wings in East Anglia: the 67th with headquarters at Walcot Hall, near Stamford; the 65th at Dane Bradbury School, Saffron Walden; and the 66th at Sawston Hall, near Cambridge. The fighters were flying from twelve airfields in Norfolk, Suffolk, Essex and Cambridgeshire.

The planes the Americans brought with them stirred great interest among those who lived near the airfields, especially schoolboys and youths with ambitions to fly, and popular imagination was stirred by the colloquial names which each of the bomb groups adopted. The 44th called themselves "The Flying Eightballs", the 91st "The Ragged Irregulars", the 92nd "Fame's Favoured Few", the 93rd "The Travelling Circus", the 303rd "Hell's Angels" and the 446th "The Bungay Buckeroos".

Many aircraft were also given names, and these were chosen—mostly by the pilot—with due regard to pictorial possibilities, so that amateur artists on the bases might decorate the fuselages with pictures. A few specimen names will suggest the flavour and the graphic possibilities: *Shady Sadie*, *Iza Vailable* and *The Urgent Virgin*. It was a special art-form, and individual servicemen achieved recognition as "New Masters" with the brush.

The Boeing B-17, better known as the "Flying Fortress", had become familiar to a few British enthusiasts during 1941 when the US sent over twenty of the early type for use by the RAF. They flew from several East Anglian bases, mainly from Polebrook, but a recognised authority on the Eighth Air Force in East Anglia recorded that "despite intensive crew training and attempts to eliminate technical troubles, it was never possible to despatch more than four Fortresses on a single operation and bombing results were always poor"[3].

The Americans had faith in them, however, and developed and improved the Fortress so that between November, 1942, and May, 1943, most USAAF bombing missions were flown by four B-17F Fortress groups, the 306th at Thurleigh, the 91st at Bassingbourn, the 303rd at Molesworth, and the 305th at Chelveston. The later versions of the plane had increased fuel capacity, better armament (twelve .50 calibre machine-guns), and superior performance all round. They were big planes: 74 feet 9 inches long, with a wing span of 103 feet 10 inches, and with the vertical fin rising 19 feet from the ground. They weighed over 60,000 lb fully loaded and carried a 5,000 lb bomb load. Despite their 4,800 hp, they were slow to take off when loaded, and made a horrendous noise as they struggled into the air at the end of the runways. Each carried a ten-man crew: pilots and engineer in the cockpit, navigator and bombardier in the nose, a radio operator, a gunner in a ball turret beneath the belly, another in the tail, and others in the waist of the ship.

A new version, the B-17G, which took the air from September, 1943, was

7

described as "the ultimate battle-worthy Fortress". Although impressive machines when seen on the ground the B-17s seemed squat compared with RAF Stirling bombers, which created an illusion that they were larger because their undercarriages were about twice as tall as those of the Fortresses. And the B-17 bomb load seemed modest beside that of the British Lancasters, which could carry seventeen 1,000 lb bombs.

The other American bombers that became familiar in East Anglia were B-24 Liberators, four-engined slab-sided planes with two large vertical fins, fewer guns but a larger bomb load, and B-26 Marauders, streamlined, cigar-shaped twin-engined medium bombers. When the first of the Marauders came to Bury St Edmunds in March with the 322nd Bomb Group they scared the inhabitants of the surrounding countryside as they practised low-level attack, skimming across the fields at breath-taking levels. One flew under an overhead power cable[4], and another ran into the ground near Cambridge and killed its crew of five. Four groups of Marauders were assigned to the Eighth Air Force, a total of 250 planes; by July, 1943, after short stays at other airfields, they were settled at four bases in Essex, Andrews Field, Earls Colne, Boxted and Chipping Ongar. In October all four groups were transferred to the Ninth Air Force.

Several new airfields were completed in the period May to July, and as they became ready the Eighth Air Force was massively reinforced until there were sixteen B-17 groups, and missions with between 200 and 300 bombers could be flown to targets deep in Germany.

Four new bomb groups arrived in the UK during April with B-17s, and six more during May, five with B-17s and one with B-26B Marauders. The size of the American air force based in Britain was thereby doubled in the course of four months, and it was announced that it would double again in the following four months.

More Fortresses arrived at Alconbury and Polebrook during May. In June two more B-17 bomb groups began operations, at Ridgewell and Grafton Underwood, and in July yet another at Framlingham, replacing a group which moved to Horham.

Bomb groups were switched around a good deal during June, frequently after only a week or a month on an airfield, so that better overall organisation was possible. A fourth wing was created, composed initially of three B-17 bomb groups, at Earls Colne, Framlingham, and Andrews Field. It was then reinforced with another bomb group at Thorpe Abbots and in July with two more at Great Ashfield and Knettishall, all flying B-17s.

By this time the surviving 1st Wing veterans were being retired from action. The assigned tour of duty for crew members was twenty-five missions, after which they could return to the United States as instructors or to take part in bond-selling (savings) campaigns, but the average life of an Eighth Air Force bomber and crew was only fifteen missions.

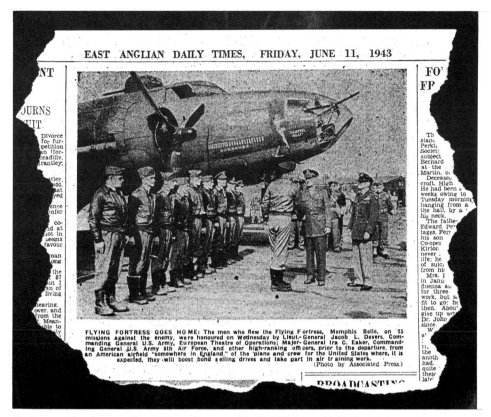

EAST ANGLIAN DAILY TIMES, FRIDAY, JUNE 11, 1943

FLYING FORTRESS GOES HOME: The men who flew the Flying Fortress, Memphis Belle, on 25 missions against the enemy, were honoured on Wednesday by Lieut-General Jacob L. Devers, Commanding General U.S. Army, European Theatre of Operations; Major-General Ira C. Eaker, Commanding General U.S. Army 8th Air Force, and other high-ranking officers, prior to the departure, from an American airfield "somewhere in England." of the plane and crew for the United States where, it is expected, they will boost bond selling drives and take part in air training work.
(Photo by Associated Press.)

Having completed twenty-five missions the crew of the B-17F "Memphis Belle" of the 91st Bomb Group at Bassingbourn returned home to America, as was reported in British newspapers at the time. The "Memphis Belle" achieved fame as the star of a film shot during actual missions.

East Anglian Daily Times

New Liberator groups arrived as the year progressed and as new bases were completed: in June at Hethel, in August at Wendling, in November at Tibenham, Bungay, and Seething, and in December at Old Buckenham. Also during December yet another group, with Fortresses, arrived at Rattlesden.

For a brief period during the summer the balance was disturbed between completion of new bases and flow of new bombers, and a number of airfields near the coast which had been designed for bombers, including Halesworth and Metfield, were temporarily assigned for fighter operations. The American fighter planes were P-38 Lightnings (which had made their debut in October, 1942) and, from April, 1943, P-47 Thunderbolts, noisy, ungainly, blunt-nosed single seaters. Neither plane had adequate range for the job in hand, and they often had to turn back just as the real enemy attacks on the bombing force began. Things improved at the end of the year, when North American P-51B Mustang IIIs arrived; these fine aircraft were an amalgamation of the American P-51 airframe and the British Rolls-Royce Merlin engine. The first was delivered to the 354th Fighter Group at Boxted in November. By the end of the year it had been followed by a dozen more.

While this dramatic build-up of American air strength took place, the Royal Air Force was also bringing into service many more, and better, planes. Technical troubles with the new Mitchell bombers were solved early in 1943 and they flew their first mission on 22nd January, attacking an oil refinery and storage tanks in Belgium.

Many of the existing force of RAF bombers were phased out: the Blenheim light bomber gave way to the Mosquito, and the Hampden and Whitley medium bombers all disappeared by January, 1943, followed by the Wellingtons late in the year. The heavy bomber force then consisted of Lancasters, Stirlings and Halifaxes, but as the months passed and Lancasters came forward from the factories in hundreds this plane became the mainstay of all operations against Germany. When there were enough of them, towards the end of the year, the Stirlings—the first RAF four-engined bomber, which had first entered service in 1940—were withdrawn from major operations. These changes called for a great deal of crew re-training. The improvement in the operationally available front-line strength of Bomber Command, both quantitatively and qualitatively, was matched by major advances in technology and technique. New radar devices made possible effective blind bombing, and great advances were made in the technique of night bombing.

Left: King George VI and Queen Elizabeth seen at RAF Coltishall during a tour of fighter stations in Norfolk during January. *Imperial War Museum*

Opposite page: Avro Lancaster bombers lined up on the airfield at Waterbeach in Cambridgeshire. *Imperial War Museum*

Almost ceaseless aerial activity over the eastern counties came to be accepted by residents as a natural part of their daily life, but the low-level practice flights caused some irritation. The *Cambridge Daily News* published a reader's letter on 14th July asking whether it was necessary for . . .

> . . . individual planes to roar a few feet overhead, possibly at dusk, waking up children or tired workers who have just gone to sleep. An afternoon has been rare on which the services in King's Chapel have not been drowned at some point in the din of planes.

The aerial operation required an enormous back-up organisation. The largest of the air bases housed three thousand personnel, forming communities larger than the quiet villages and small towns to which, almost overnight it seemed, they had become close neighbours. They were served by an endless stream of trucks and trains, bringing bombs and ammunition and the supplies required for the routines of daily life. Support staffs scurried around the country lanes in RAF trucks and USAAF jeeps, and "liberty trucks" took the men into the nearest towns every night in search of amusement.

It added up to a revolution in the life of the region, and it was a revolution that had not run its course as 1943 came to a close. More airfields were still being built: at Beccles, Birch, Boreham, Butley, Debach, Deopham Green, Ely, Eye, Glatton (Hunts), Gosfield, Hadstock, Hepworth, Lavenham, Matching, Mepal (Cambs), Nuthampstead, Pickenham, Rackheath, Stansted Mountfitchet, Tuddenham and Winfarthing[5]. East Anglia, beyond question, was the biggest "flight deck" the world had ever seen.

RAF AIRFIELDS AND AIRCRAFT IN EAST ANGLIA, 1943

BOMBER COMMAND (No 2 GROUP)

Attlebridge	Mitchells	**Oulton**	Bostons & Venturas
Docking	Wellingtons & Venturas	**Sculthorpe**	Bostons & Mosquitoes
Foulsham	Mitchells	**Swanton Morley**	Mitchells, Bostons &
Great Massingham	Wellingtons & Bostons		Mosquitoes
Hunsdon	Venturas	**West Raynham**	Mitchells, Bostons,
Marham	Mosquitoes		Hurricanes &
Methwold	Mitchells & Venturas		Mosquitoes

BOMBER COMMAND (No 3 GROUP)

Bourn	Lancasters	**Newmarket**	Stirlings
Chedburgh	Stirlings	**Ridgewell**	Stirlings
Downham Market	Stirlings	**Stradishall**	Stirlings
East Wretham	Lancasters	**Tempsford**	Special Operations
Feltwell	Wellingtons	**Tuddenham**	Stirlings & Lancasters
Gransden Lodge	Special Operations	**Upwood**	Halifaxes & Lancasters
Lakenheath	Wellingtons & Stirlings	**Waterbeach**	Stirlings
Little Snoring	Lancasters	**Wethersfield**	Stirlings
Mepal	Stirlings	**Witchford (Ely)**	Stirlings & Lancasters
Mildenhall	Stirlings	**Wratting Common**	Stirlings

BOMBER COMMAND PATHFINDER FORCE (No 8 GROUP)

Graveley	Halifaxes	**Warboys**	Lancasters.
Oakington	Stirlings & Lancasters	**Wyton**	Lancasters & Mosquitoes

AIR DEFENCE OF GREAT BRITAIN: FIGHTER COMMAND

Bradwell Bay	Spitfires, Mosquitoes & Typhoons	**Ludham**	Spitfires
		Matlaske	Typhoons
Castle Camps	Mosquitoes	**Snailwell**	Typhoons & Mustangs
Coltishall	Spitfires & Typhoons		

OTHER RAF BASES OPERATIONAL DURING 1943

Bircham Newton	Coastal Command	**Woodbridge**	Emergency landing field
Felixstowe	Catalina flying boat maintenance base		

USAAF AIRFIELDS IN EAST ANGLIA, 1943

Airfield	*Date occupied by USAAF*	*Unit*	*Aircraft*	*Period of occupation*
BOMBER BASES				
Grafton Underwood (3½ miles north of Kettering)	May, 1942	97th BG	B-17E	7/42–9/42
		305th BG	B-17	9/42–12/42
		96th BG	B-17	4/43–5/43
		384th BG	B-17F	5/43–6/45

Chelveston (5 miles east of Welling- borough)	June, 1942	60th Troop Carrier Group 301st BG 305th BG	C-47 B-17 B-17	7/42 8/42–11/42 12/42–7/45
Molesworth (10½ miles west of Huntingdon)	June, 1942 (ex-RAF)	15th BS 303rd BG	Bostons B-17	6/42–9/42 9/42–6/45
Polebrook (2 miles south-east of Oundle)	Summer, 1942 (ex-RAF)	97th BG 351st BG	B-17E B-17F	6/42–10/42 4/43–6/45
Alconbury	Sept, 1942 (ex-RAF)	93rd BG 92nd BG 95th BG 482nd BG	B-24 B-17 B-17 B-17F	9/42–12/42 1/43–9/43 4/43–6/43 8/43–6/45
Bury St Edmunds (Rougham)	Sept, 1942	47th BG 322nd BG 94th BG	A-20B B-26B B-17	9/42–10/42 12/42–6/43 6/43–12/45
Hardwick (5½ miles west of Bungay)	Sept, 1942	310th BG 93rd BG	B-25 B-24D	9/42–11/42 12/42–6/45
Kimbolton	Sept, 1942	91st BG 17th BG 379th BG	B-17 B-17	9/42–10/42 10/42–11/42 5/43–6/45
Podington (near Bedford)	Sept, 1942	15th BS 301st BG 100th BG 92nd BG	Bostons B-17 B-17 B-17	9/42–11/42 8/42–9/42 6/43 9/43–7/45
Thurleigh (5 miles north of Bedford)	Sept, 1942 (ex-RAF)	306th BG	B-17	9/42–12/45
Bassingbourn (3½ miles north of Royston)	Oct, 1942 (pre-war, ex-RAF)	91st BG 94th BG	B-17 B-17	10/42–6/45 4/43–5/43
Horham (near Eye)	Oct, 1942	47th BG 95th BG 323rd BG	A-20B B-17F B-26C	10/42–1/43 6/43–8/45 5/43–6/43
Shipdham (3 miles south of East Dereham)	Oct, 1942	44th BG	B-24	10/42–6/45
Bungay (Flixton)	Nov, 1942	310th BG 93rd BG 446th BG	(one sqdn) B-25C (one sqdn) B-24 B-24H	11/42 12/42–3/43 11/43–7/45
Hethel (7 miles south-west of Norwich)	Nov, 1942	320th BG 389th BG	 B-24D	11/42 6/43–5/45
Rattlesden (between Stowmarket & Bury St Edmunds)	Dec, 1942	322nd BG 447th BG	B-26C B-17G	12/42–4/43 11/43–8/45

Andrews Field (Gt Saling) (4 miles west-north-west of Braintree)	May, 1943	96th BG 322nd BG	B-17 B-26C	5/43–6/43 6/43–9/44
Earls Colne	May, 1943	94th BG 323rd BG	B-17 B-26B and B-26C	5/43–6/43 6/43–7/44
Framlingham	May, 1943	95th BG 390th BG	B-17 B-17F	5/43–6/43 7/43–8/45
Boxted	June, 1943	386th BG	B-26B/C	6/43–9/43
Chipping Ongar	June, 1943	387th BG	B-26B	6/43–7/44
Great Ashfield (10 miles east of Bury St Edmunds)	June, 1943	385th BG	B-17F	6/43–8/45
Great Dunmow	June, 1943	386th BG	B-26B	9/43–10/44
Knettishall (5 miles east-south-east of Thetford)	June, 1943	388th BG	B-17F	6/43–8/45
Ridgewell (near Haverhill)	June, 1943 (ex-RAF)	381st BG	B-17	6/43–6/45
Snetterton Heath (6 miles south-west of Attleborough)	June, 1943	386th BG 96th BG	B-26B B-17F	6/43 6/43–12/45
Thorpe Abbots (between Diss & Harleston)	June, 1943	100th BG	B-17	6/43–12/45
Wendling 4 miles west-north-west of East Dereham)	Aug, 1943	392nd BG	B-24H	8/43–6/45
Tibenham (13½ miles south-south-west of Norwich)	Nov, 1942	445th BG	B-24H	11/43–5/45
Deenethorpe (Northants)	Nov, 1943	401st BG	B-17G	11/43–6/45

An informal photograph of Air Vice-Marshal J. H. D'Albiac and Brigadier-General Robert Candee enjoying tea and doughnuts at an American Red Cross mobile canteen after the handing over of an RAF airfield to the USAAF. *East Anglian Daily Times*

Seething (9½ miles south-east of Norwich)	Nov, 1943	448th BG	B-24H	11/43–7/45
Old Buckenham (2 miles south-east of Attleborough)	Dec, 1943	453rd BG	B-24H	12/43–5/45

FIGHTER BASES

Horsham St Faiths	Sept, 1942 (ex-RAF)	56th FG	P-47	4/43–7/43
Debden	Sept, 1942 (pre-war, ex-RAF)	4th FG	Spitfires/P-47	9/42–7/45
Duxford	Oct, 1942 (pre-war, ex-RAF)	350th FG 78th FG	P-39 P-47C	10/42–1/43 6/43–10/45
Bodney (between Swaffham & Brandon)	July, 1943 (ex-RAF)	352nd FG	P-47D	7/43–2/45
Halesworth	July, 1943	56th FG	P-47	7/43–4/44
Steeple Morden (3½ miles west of Royston)	July, 1943 (ex-RAF)	355th FG	P-47D	7/43–7/45
Metfield (between Halesworth & Harleston)	Aug, 1943	353rd FG	P-47D	8/43–4/44
East Wretham (6 miles north-east of Thetford)	Oct, 1943 (ex-RAF)	359th FG	P-47D	10/43–11/45
Boxted		354th FG	P-51B	11/43–4/44
Martlesham Heath (3 miles north-east of Ipswich)	Oct, 1943 (pre-war, ex-RAF)	356th FG	P-47D	10/43–11/45
Bottisham (between Cambridge & Newmarket)	Nov, 1943 (ex-RAF)	361st FG	P-47D	11/43–9/44
Leiston	Nov, 1943	358th FG	P-47D	11/43–2/44
Raydon	Nov, 1943	357th FG	P-47 & P-51B	11/43–1/44

MAINTENANCE BASES

Honington (between Bury & Thetford)	Summer, 1942 (pre-war, ex-RAF)	1st Strategic Air Depot for B-17 Fortresses of the Eighth Air Force.
Wattisham (9 miles north-west of Ipswich)	1942 (pre-war, ex-RAF)	USAAF air depot from 1942, servicing many types of aircraft, but by late 1943 concentrat- ing on fighters.
Watton	1943 (ex-RAF)	3rd Strategic Air Depot for B-24 Liberators of the 2nd Air Division.

CHAPTER TWO

The Roar of Allied Bombers

THERE had been a transformation in the general war situation. After the defeats of 1940, the desperate struggle during 1941 to "hold on", and the slow rebuilding of confidence and of strength during 1942 as Russia and America went on to the offensive, the New Year offered hope of bold and positive action by the combined Allies, with British forces more fully deployed. Perhaps, indeed, this was going to be the year of the great invasion of Europe, the so-called "Second Front", and the collapse of Germany; even, some dared to hope, of a victorious end to the war.

The prelude to invasion, the war chiefs decided, must be a massive aerial bombardment of the enemy's factories and cities to destroy his productive capacity and to undermine his morale. The RAF had begun this assault during 1942 with its Stirling and Lancaster bombers, flying at night and attempting "saturation bombing" of German cities, and it had managed several thousand-bomber raids.

These operations were supplemented from August, 1942, by the United States Army Air Force in East Anglia, but the Americans flew only by day, and when the year ended their planes had yet to cross the German frontier. They made twenty-six raids in all, but only eight during November and four during December, and thirty-three bombers and nine fighters had been lost in action. Poor visibility had led to the cancellation of many planned operations. British defence chiefs felt disappointed about the build-up and the performance of the American air fleet.

At the Churchill–Roosevelt conference in Casablanca in mid-January, 1943, there was a confrontation between the British Prime Minister and the commander of the Eighth, Brigadier-General Ira Eaker. Churchill's doubts about the whole strategy of daylight bombing, to which the Americans were firmly wedded, were forcefully expressed:

> It was certainly a terrible thing that in the whole of the last six months of 1942 nothing had come of this immense deployment and effort—not a single bomb had been dropped on Germany. There must have been twenty thousand men and five hundred machines all laid out in East Anglia, and nothing so far, as it seemed, to show for it all.[1]

General Eaker prevailed on Churchill to be patient, and almost immediately

Opposite page: Pilots of the 353rd Fighter Group are briefed at Metfield before setting out in support of a bombing mission. Two cords stretching from Metfield mark their outward and homeward courses; the third cord marks the route of the bomber force.   *Robert Strobell*

A formation of Consolidated B-24D Liberators of the 8th USAAF over East Anglian fields. Formations were designed to enable air gunners to provide maximum defensive fire against enemy fighters.

Imperial War Museum

he stepped up the aerial offensive, starting with an attack by fifty-three Flying Fortresses on the naval base at Wilhelmshaven on 27th January. Thereafter British and American bomber forces maintained a continuous joint assault on the Nazi heartland, steadily increasing the number of planes despatched and the depth of penetration.

The RAF bombing campaign had all along been based upon a directive of February, 1942, which emphasised that it should be "focused on the morale of the enemy civil population and, in particular, of the industrial workers"[2]. This was the purpose of the thousand-bomber raids, but their effectiveness was debatable and when the loss of planes rose to almost five per cent by June they were abandoned*. Bomber Command lost 1,404 planes in action, and 2,724 others were damaged, so that by January, 1943, the daily average of bombers available for operations was only 515. Of the 336 heavy bombers, more than 120 were obsolescent Wellingtons.

The US bomber force had from its establishment specialised in high-level

*Subsequent evidence showed that they did not seriously affect German war production, which rose by 50 per cent during 1942. (Ref: B. H. Liddell Hart: *History of the Second World War*, Cassell, 1970, page 599).

daylight bombing, concentrated on carefully-selected industrial and economic targets, seeking to disorganise enemy war production. The Americans believed they had the equipment to achieve the necessary precision to do this. The British, on the other hand, held to their conviction that it was better to seek "such a general degree of devastation in all the major towns that organised industrial activity would cease, owing to a combination of material and moral effects". The result was that "for most of 1943 there was no combined offensive, but on the contrary, a bombing competition"[3].

The Casablanca conference produced a new directive which sought to unify these different philosophies:

> The progressive destruction and dislocation of the German military, industrial and economic system, and the undermining of the morale of the German people to a point where their capacity for armed resistance is fatally weakened.

The assault was developed week by week on Germany and the occupied countries, plus a sustained effort to cripple German naval forces that were threatening Allied shipping in the Atlantic. During 1942 Axis submarines had sunk 1,160 Allied vessels, totalling 6,266,000 tons, and losses were continuing at an alarming level. At 1st January, 1943, the Germans had 212 U-boats at sea, compared with only ninety-one a year earlier. Until the Battle of the Atlantic had been won, there could be no question of attempting an invasion of Europe, and it was not until the end of March, 1943, that this shipping crisis receded.

Liberators of the 93rd Bomb Group at Hardwick flew many of the missions against U-boat pens at St Nazaire, Lorient and other Atlantic ports. They joined in a "maximum effort" raid on the U-boat construction yards at Vegesack on the Weser on 27th January which was part of the first American raid on Germany; this assault was made by sixty-four Fortresses from Thurleigh, Molesworth, Chelveston, Bassingbourn and Shipdham, led by the 306th Bomb Group from Thurleigh.

Berlin was first raided in daylight by three Mosquitoes of RAF Bomber Command which flew from Marham, in Norfolk, on 30th January—ten years to the day after Hitler had been sworn in as Chancellor of Nazi Germany. They arrived over the German capital at precisely 11 am, dropped their bombs, and returned safely to Marham. The raid was timed to coincide with a radio broadcast by Hermann Goering, head of the Luftwaffe; it forced him to postpone his performance for an hour. This was a useful propaganda coup, capturing front-page headlines, as in the *Cambridge Daily News*:

BERLIN BOMBED TODAY

Mosquitoes cut in on Anniversary

Goering's speech held up an hour

But when three other Mosquitoes from Marham attempted to disrupt a 4 pm speech by the German propaganda chief, Josef Goebbels, Luftwaffe fighters were waiting for them and shot one down.

Attacks on naval bases continued. On 1st March the *East Anglian Daily Times*, reporting raids by US Fortresses and Liberators on Brest and by RAF Venturas on Dunkirk, summed up:

> When the last of the big forces of RAF and US bomber and fighter planes landed at their bases on Saturday night, after daylight raids on the German U-boat base at Brest and the harbour at Dunkirk, the most devastating and intensified bombing offensive of the war from Britain had been in progress for sixty hours.

The next day front-page headlines told of another big raid on a naval target:

1,000 TONS OF BOMBS ON U-BOAT BASE

Defences swamped at St Nazaire

PORT A MASS OF FLAMES

In the first five months of 1943 British and American bombers aimed nearly 20,000 tons of high explosives and incendiaries on the U-boat bases and building yards, but, despite the newspaper headlines, it had little effect on the enemy*. Sinkings of Atlantic convoy vessels escalated in February and March; in one convoy twenty-one ships were sunk for the loss of only one U-boat. When the tide turned, during the spring, it was due to technical advances by Allied scientists and the availability of more escort destroyers and more long-range Liberators to provide air cover. U-boat losses went up to a level which the Germans could not face and so by July, for the first time, more Allied ships were built than were sunk.

None of these problems and dangers were disclosed to the public at the time. The diet of newspaper headlines was consistently propagandist. On 3rd March the *East Anglian Daily Times* front page was headed:

BERLIN GETS HEAVIEST BOMBING OF THE WAR

R.A.F. shower biggest bombs on blazing German capital

In fact, the opening months of 1943 were a relatively quiet period for the RAF, compared with 1942, as crews were accustoming themselves to the Lancasters and Mosquitoes which were replacing the older bombers in increasing numbers.

When the Air Minister, Sir Archibald Sinclair, introduced the Air Estimates in the Commons on 11th March he reported that Bomber Command had destroyed or seriously damaged something like two thousand factories and industrial works.

The Member of Parliament for Ipswich, Mr Richard Stokes, had already established a reputation as a vigorous critic of "saturation bombing", and he now

---

*After the war, the official naval history stated that not a single U-boat was put out of action and there was no appreciable effect on the German building programme. (Ref: Roskill, Capt. S. W.: *The War at Sea, 1939–45*, vol. 2, page 352.)

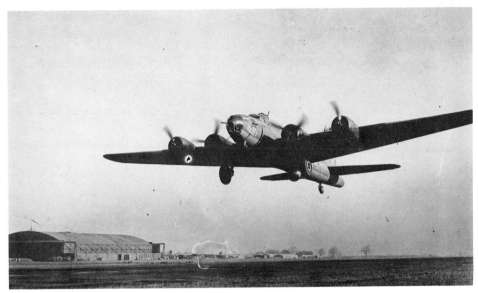

American combat crews chose what they thought appropriate names for their "ships". This B-17F taking off from an East Anglian base is named "Knock-out Dropper".   *Imperial War Museum*

renewed his attack. "I want to protest against the steady destruction of Europe by bombing," he told a House of Commons in which there were few prepared to support him. "I recognise the gallantry of the men who do it, and I am sure a lot of them don't like it, but I feel sick with nausea when I think of the destruction of Europe and I am not in the least compensated when I am told that Hitler intended to destroy London."

Public reaction to the raids was mixed, and some agreed with Richard Stokes, but during the early months of the year the main reactions were either excitement at the thought that the Allies were at last hitting back or apprehension that the Allied raids would bring reprisals. A Sheringham diarist, Mrs Sarah Williams, noted in January:

> Everybody here is terribly agitated because of the bombing of Berlin, and bolts into a shelter immediately an aeroplane is heard. Several of them say that they wish it hadn't happened.

In March William Stock, a Chelmsford shop assistant, noted:

> The fact that we are making terrific bombing raids on Germany doesn't make everybody happy. My sister said: "I think we shall get some bad air-raids before long." Personally, I abhor this gloating over the extent of our bombing . . .

In the Commons the Under Secretary for Air, Captain Balfour, replied to

Richard Stokes: "Our objectives are, as they always have been, the industry, transport and war potential of our enemy . . . If, in the pursuit of our objectives, the German civilian population has to suffer, it is not our fault. It is not for us to turn back because of that. The remedy lies in the hands of the German people themselves." This doubtless expressed the majority feeling in the country, and he was cheered by the House.

The foremost proponent of saturation bombing, Air Chief Marshal Sir Arthur Harris, developed the RAF's aerial assault in three main phases, beginning in March, 1943, with the "Battle of the Ruhr", extending in the summer months to the "Battle of Hamburg", and culminating in the "Battle of Berlin", beginning in November. The official war history declares that "their object was the devastation of the greatest possible acreage in the most heavily built-up areas"[4].

In the end, both British and American bombing theories were disproved. The Germans were not so affected by heavy bombing that they ceased to offer resistance, and their production of armaments actually increased by leaps and bounds during this period[5]. Before the year was out the Americans reached the point at which they could no longer afford the losses entailed in their style of attack. The people of East Anglia who watched the bombers depart, and noted that many

Badly shot up during a raid on Bremen on 8th October, B-17F "Just a-Snappin" of the 100th Bomb Group based at Thorpe Abbots crash-landed at Ludham on its return.

Major-General J. B. Kidd, USAF

returned with heavy damage or did not return at all, were witnessing a tragic drama: so much wilful theorising, so much effort, so much sacrifice, for so little result.

The roar of aircraft engines was unceasing in the eastern counties. In Sheringham Mrs Sarah Williams . . .

> . . . watched seventy-one Flying Fortresses leaving for Germany. Went to the pictures during the evening . . . At times the speech was drowned by the roar of our bombers going out . . .

Some of the American daylight raids were made at a grievous price. In April a force of 107 B-17s was sent to attack an aircraft factory at Bremen; sixteen were shot down, and that meant the loss of 160 highly-trained flyers. These human losses caused serious problems. When a dozen new Liberators arrived at Shipdham during April there were insufficient trained men available to put them into the air, and crews were borrowed from the RAF and from Fortress groups.

In Washington in May—by which time it was clear that the strength of the Luftwaffe was actually increasing, despite the bombing—the Allied leaders decided that the primary objective of future bombing must be destruction of the Luftwaffe and the German aircraft industry. At this stage the Eighth Army Air Force had made thirty attacks, and the question remained: Could its bombers make effective daylight raids without prohibitive losses?

The assault was sustained and developed, with greater co-ordination of British and American efforts. There was a series of forty-three raids on targets in the Ruhr between March and July. Advances were made in bombing technique, but the loss of planes remained serious.

May saw one of the most daring RAF exploits, resulting in the destruction of two of Germany's greatest dams, the Möhne and Eder. Also in May there was a disastrous raid by a dozen Venturas based at Methwold, Norfolk, on steelworks at Ijmuiden in Holland. They were due to rendezvous with escort fighters over Flushing, but the fighters arrived on the scene early, became involved in dog-fights and, with fuel running low, had to return before the British bombers arrived. When they did, the Luftwaffe was waiting for them and shot down all but one, which limped home badly damaged[6].

On 14th May the USAAF, with reinforcements arriving in East Anglia almost weekly, was able to despatch more than two hundred heavy bombers against enemy targets for the first time. By 13th June, when three of the most recently arrived bomb groups completed their first month of combat operations, they had lost more than two hundred men and twenty planes in eight missions. As this tally was being counted, there were twenty-two more losses in a raid on Kiel, so that after only nine missions nearly half the original crews and aircraft had been lost. At Framlingham the 95th Bomb Group lost ten of its planes, and 102 men. One of those who got back afterwards related that "following a thoroughly depressing and sad debriefing, during which he listened to the accounts of the surviving crews in silence, Colonel Kessler, his eyes brimming with tears and very obviously extremely distressed, could only murmur, to no-one in particular: 'What's happened to my boys? What's happened to my boys?' "[7]

RAF Bomber Command's offensive reached a new peak in June, when 15,000 tons of bombs were dropped in twenty nights, compared with 12,500 tons in May and 10,000 tons in April.

Between July and November there were thirty-three major attacks on the Hamburg area, in some of which the USAAF joined forces with the RAF. William Stock recorded his views in his diary:

> There is something shocking about raids on Hamburg. It is no good being soft-hearted about war, but one can't help imagining the terror of those awful assaults on an already much-bombed town. Press and radio now openly gloat over the fearful air attacks being made on German and Italian towns. These terrific assaults may be an essential part of our strategy, but there is no need to be so pleased about it. One cannot think of the effect of these raids without a feeling of solemnity.

In August and September, heavy bombers joined with B-26 Marauders to attack airfields and communication centres in France and the Low Countries as part of a ruse to make the Germans fear a full-scale invasion, to try to deter them from moving troops to Russia and Italy.

For a few months the bases at Hardwick, Hethel and Shipdham went quiet. Four new squadrons of Liberators flew into Hethel from the United States during June and spent the following two weeks in co-operation with Liberators at Shipdham and Hardwick practising wing-tip to wing-tip flying at only 150 feet. There was one mid-air collision near the Hardwick base in which a crewman died and two were injured. All this was in preparation for a raid on oilfields at Ploesti in Rumania. The three groups, with 124 Liberators, flew to Libya at the end of the month, from there flew several missions in support of the Italian campaign, bombed Ploesti on 1st August, and returned to East Anglia during the last week of August. They were hardly back. however, before they were ordered to return to Africa to support Allied landings on the Italian mainland at Salerno. They had returned to East Anglia again by October.

William Stock's diary entry contrasted sharply with his view of the Hamburg raids:

> The raid on the Ploesti oilfields is a good example of a daring and telling attack on a vital strategic target.

General Eaker, commander of the Eighth Army Air Force, decided at this time to make an all-out effort to bomb crucial industrial targets in Germany. On 17th August a force of three hundred planes attacked the Messerschmitt factory at Regensburg and a ball-bearing factory at Schweinfurt—the deepest penetration into Germany that the Eighth Army Air Force had attempted. Sixty of those planes did not return.

One hundred Ridgewell men were lost. The chaplain of the base noted that evening: "Ridgewell Aerodrome . . . is like a city morgue"[8]. A crew member among those who got back wrote:

> Morning brought a severe letdown in morale. At breakfast very few men showed up . . . The usual chatter and banter was absent. Men ate in silence and left quickly. I found myself looking around for faces that I knew that I would never see again.[9]

It took a month to rebuild at Ridgewell, and for the Eighth Air Force to come back to strength. Four months later, on 2nd December, two of the missing men who had evaded capture when their plane was shot down at Schweinfurt walked on to the Ridgewell base. With only a compass, living on root vegetables, they had made their way out of Germany into France; there the French underground had taken them under its wing and smuggled them to England. The chaplain at Ridgewell, the Reverend James Good Brown, kept a daily diary, and that night he wrote in it:

> The whole place was ablaze with interest . . The men literally go wild with joy. It is a sign that fliers who go down in combat have a chance to escape from the Continent, or at least escape with their lives.[10]

On the night after the Americans bombed Schweinfurt and Regensburg six hundred bombers from many East Anglian bases raided the flying bomb research and experimental station at Peenemunde, on the Baltic coast. Forty were shot down by anti-aircraft guns, fifteen crashed on the return journey, and seventeen others were damaged.

When the short summer nights began to lengthen, the RAF began to raid Berlin more often. The *East Anglian Daily Times* described the events of Monday 23rd August:

> Air Chief Marshal Sir Arthur Harris, Bomber Command chief, has launched the long nights' battle of Berlin with the most devastating aerial bombardment that has ever shattered a capital. On Monday night something like 700 of Britain's biggest bombers smashed through the greatest fighter screen the Germans could put into the night sky over the Reich to crash 1,700 tons of bombs on Berlin in about fifty minutes.

Despite this hyperbole, in three raids on the German capital the Allies lost 123 bombers. It did not deter the air chiefs, for they continued the regular attacks on the city despite continuing losses, and Harris held doggedly to his view that aerial assault alone would defeat Germany*. A force of 338 Flying Fortresses attacked a factory at Stuttgart on 6th September, and forty-five of them were lost, wiping out completely the 563rd squadron at Knettishall. The attack was sustained, and by October Allied bombers ranged over almost every corner of Europe, the daylight efforts of the American planes matched by those of RAF Lancasters, Stirlings and Halifaxes flying from Coningsby, Feltwell, Great Massingham, Oakington, Scampton, Waterbeach and many other bases.

---

*The saturation raids were eventually abandoned in March, 1944, when it was at last conceded that the losses were unacceptable.

General Eaker resolved to make another bold attempt to strike the industrial area of Bremen, and his decision opened a critical week of the war. He sent four hundred bombers to attack the city on 8th October. The cost to the Eighth Air Force was thirty-one aircraft. At Ridgewell, where the 381st Bomb Group lost seven planes, and other of its crews died in planes that managed to struggle back, the Reverend James Good Brown summed up sadly:

> We arrived here June 5, 1943. We flew our first mission June 22, 1943. We had lost half our Group by August 17th, Schweinfurt, Germany. We had lost the other half by October 8th and 9th in the Bremen and Anklam raids. From here on, we were an entirely new outfit. The name 381st remains the same. The flying personnel is different. No longer can it be looked upon as a family . . . Replacements now come in almost every day, and before we learn to know them, they have gone down in combat . . .[11]

Things went very badly that week. On 10th October sixteen bomb groups were despatched to Munster. It was a raid about which there were some misgivings

Their posture might seem relaxed, but the strain shows on the faces of 390th Bomb Group aircrew as they listen to an early-morning briefing at Framlingham.　　　　*USAF*

before it began. At the briefing of their 95th Bomb Group at Horham, the Intelligence Officer announced:

> Unlike all previous military and industrial targets attacked to date, today it will be different, very different, because today you will hit the centre of the city, the homes of the working population . . .

Some of the crews who heard these words had troubled thoughts. One officer, who was to fly as a navigator, approached his commanding officer when he learned that the aiming point for this Sunday afternoon raid would be the main entrance to Munster Cathedral. He explained that he came from a strict Protestant background, and said he would prefer not to fly. His CO responded: "You have no option. If you do not fly, I'll have to court-martial you." In this raid the Americans met almost impossible odds over Germany and lost thirty Fortresses[12].

Then came "Black Thursday", 14th October, when the Eighth Air Force sent out 291 Fortresses, one task force led by the 96th Bomb Group from Snetterton, on deep penetration raids. It lost sixty-two of them and only thirty came back undamaged. Altogether, in that single week, the USAAF lost 148 planes.

No-one reading the newspapers or listening to the radio would have guessed the harsh truth, which can rarely be told in wartime. The *East Anglian Daily Times* reported on 25th October that "Allied bombers were over Germany, Austria, Hungary and Yugoslavia in daylight yesterday" and headlined its main front-page story:

BERLIN'S 5,000 TONS IN THREE NIGHTS

Most-bombed City

Though unaware of the cost in Allied lives, there were people who were perturbed by the scale of the raids. A fifty-year-old retired science mistress living in East Bergholt indicated how some were torn with their emotions when she wrote towards the end of the year:

> I feel very unhappy about the recent bombing of Germany. I know it is the "fault" of the Germans themselves. They "began" it. But, all the same, I cannot help thinking of the destitution we are causing, the chaos and the human misery and hopelessness. This may be mere sentimentality, I know. I also feel so terribly sorry for all our young airmen, who have to undergo these terrible hazards on our behalf. What they endure for us we can never fully appreciate, and I am sure that all the destruction they have to accomplish is really grim for them too. But if it hastens the end of the war, I suppose it is therefore justified. As a humanitarian, one loathes it, but war knows no humanitarianism.[13]

The US Eighth Army Air Force effort slackened towards the end of the year and its losses in December were about one in thirty of the planes it sent out, compared with nearly one in ten of those that flew during October.

Many of these heavy bomber raids on German targets were given direct support by RAF Typhoons, which ranged over and near the bombers' flight paths to engage and divert Luftwaffe fighters. Later the Typhoons made regular low-level

Squadron Leader Ron Hawkins, who was lost as he led his Typhoon squadron on a raid in October. He had been chief flying instructor at Ipswich Airport before the war.
Mr Ian Hawkins

attacks on industrial plants and communications centres in France and the Low Countries. It was in one of these raids that one of East Anglia's most distinguished flyers lost his life: Squadron Leader Ron Hawkins, MC, AFC, who at the outbreak of war had been chief flying instructor at Ipswich Airport. Hawkins had been shot down before, in June, 1940, soon after the British withdrawal from Dunkirk, while he was bombing pontoon bridges over the River Meuse in German-occupied France. On that occasion he parachuted from his plane, was captured by the Germans, escaped, and made a long, lone trek across France and over the Pyrenees into Spain, and so back to England. He may have been the first RAF aircrew to complete this journey, and the detailed notes he supplied to the Air Ministry on his return proved of great value in developing what later became the principal escape route. By 1943 Hawkins was commanding officer of No 3 Squadron (Typhoons) at Manston, Kent. Early in October he led a raid on a petroleum refinery near Ghent, and his was one of two RAF planes shot down.

By that time the British had a new anxiety. Reconnaissance had revealed the existence of eighty-eight launching sites on the Continent for pilotless "flying bombs", and there was evidence to suggest that there might be about fifty more of them. From November, 1943, fighter-bombers of the RAF 2nd Tactical Air Force concentrated on attacking these launching sites in northern France, aided by strong

Accommodation on the airfields constructed for the USAAF was mainly in huts, but efforts were made by the occupants to improve their surroundings. This mural is on the wall of a nissen hut at Horham in Suffolk. *Mary Hawkins*

forces of US Fortresses and Liberators. Briefing the crews of Liberators at Wendling when they joined one of these attacks two days before Christmas, an Intelligence Officer declared that the coming invasion of Europe could well be delayed if these sites were not knocked out; apart from which, he added, "If these sites are not destroyed within the next three months London will be totally devastated"[14].

This preoccupation, and the approach of the Christmas season, did not deflect the air chiefs from their campaign against German industrial targets. Leverkusen was bombed by the Eighth Army Air Force on 1st December, and Bremen on the 16th and 20th. The Ridgewell bomb group joined all these raids. In the first it lost four combat crews, forty men; in the second its planes were unscathed; in the third the group again lost four planes and forty men. The chaplain wrote that night:

> Our luck had been good since December 1st. Twenty days without a loss gave us a kind of reprieve and lifted our spirits, as we approached the Christmas season. Today's losses convince us that this war is a grim business. I do not welcome the task of writing letters of condolence to all those families announcing this sad news five days before Christmas.[15]

Bad weather on Christmas Day and for several days afterwards prevented flying, so the next mission for the Ridgewell men was on 30th December, to

Ludwigshaven. All thirty-three planes returned safely, and with this raid thirteen men finished their twenty-five required missions. In a matter of days, grief was followed by jubilation, emphasising the hazards of fate.

The US bases were unlike RAF stations. James Good Brown wrote:

> The fliers have no resemblance to soldiers. We are, rather, a bunch of specialised workers—a group of technicians . . . We do not even think of ourselves as soldiers. The actions of the men are generally unmilitary. There are no marches. There is no drilling. Men look like workers in a factory, or office men in an insurance company.[16]

The Americans usually bombed by day, but their missions left at many different hours around the clock, so that the life of a base was non-stop, day and night. When there was a mission, a sergeant would do a round of the huts waking those who were to fly, perhaps as early as 4 am. After a quick breakfast, briefing followed at perhaps 5.30 am, and takeoff would then be at 6.30 am. Fliers attending a typical Eighth Army Air Force briefing would probably arrive at the Nissen hut in trucks, file into the building in silence, and sit on backless benches. They would be wearing their heavy fur-lined, electrically-heated flying clothes—at the 20,000 to 27,000 feet altitude at which the B-17s flew, temperatures in the planes could drop to −50°C. Facing them would probably be their commanding officer, deputy commander, and operations officer. The chaplain was usually there, too, to speak uplifting words, possibly a prayer[17].

The Reverend James Good Brown vividly described such a briefing, at 2.30 am on 14th December, 1943:

> When the men enter the room, they immediately look up to see the board which shows who is flying and in what position. Sighs are heard. They look to see who is flying in "coffin's corner"—out in the wings—or in the tail position. After much chatter and comment, for they do not know yet where they are going (the movie screen is pulled down over the map on the wall in front of the room), the Commanding Officer looks on the chart and calls the roll of pilots. Each pilot responds, and when he does, it indicates that his whole crew is present . . .
>
> Then the screen is rolled up, and there is revealed the map with the red cord leading from Ridgewell, Essex, England, to the place of the mission. This day it was Berlin . . . When the men saw the word "Berlin" they gave a large groan . . . The screen is rolled down and the projector casts on the screen the pictures of the target.[18]

At Ridgewell pilots and navigators attended the briefings and the gunners went ahead to check the planes. Before doing so

> . . . one of us would stand outside the door of the Briefing Room. As soon as the curtain covering the target map was pulled back the reactions of the officers could be plainly heard; that told us about how rough the target was going to be . . .[19]

The Intelligence Officer described the target as shown on the screen, gave the lie of the land, identified landmarks, and announced that the MPI (maximum point of impact) was to be the Air Ministry headquarters in Berlin. He showed still pictures, day-maps and night-maps, prepared on the basis of reconnaissance, and then showed the course to be taken, indicating areas where anti-aircraft flak might be expected, the probable intensity of which was shown by the density of red spots.

The weatherman followed, reporting on visibility, cloud conditions and temperature, and the radio officer, telling what signals to use. The commanding officer gave an assessment of the number of fighters they might encounter on the way, and reported how many Fortresses would be involved altogether, and the number of friendly fighters that would accompany them. Finally, the call signals were given, and there was a time check.

If, after the briefing, the men had time to kill before takeoff, they would sit in groups chatting nostalgically about their home towns or what kind of car they might buy after the war; or they would stretch out on benches, recalling past adventures

Lieutenant John Pettinger and his crew pose in front of their B-17 "The Vibrant Virgin". The crew survived when their aircraft was shot down on 10th October, and all became prisoners of war.

John Pettinger

and speculating about the future; or, on cold nights, they would gather around the stove, re-living earlier raids. Finally, when the hour came:

> . . . Shoulder to shoulder, we walk out together. It is good to hop on the truck with them, going out to the planes. In the darkness of the night in the back of the truck there may be no word spoken. In silence we ride to where the plane is parked . . . The engines start. The fog is lifting. The zero hour approaches. The plane slowly moves away from its station.[20]

James Good Brown noted that the briefing of a new group of flyers embarking on their first combat mission had a special quality, and when the 381st Bomb Group arrived at Ridgewell early in the summer of 1943 he attended its first briefing and that same evening committed these impressions to his diary:

> They try to joke, but it is artificial. They are resolute. They talk freely of the Jerries, but they do not yet know what they are talking about. They say "This is the real thing". But they do not yet know what "real" means. They look happy and free. But they admit they are like scared rats. They say "There's nothing to it". There is no describing the varied reactions. Each man has a million reactions. The briefing room is a mass of contradictions. The one thing in common seems to be "fear of death". "I do not want to die".[21]

Once airborne, the bombers needed sixty to ninety minutes to assemble in formation. Taking off at fixed intervals of thirty or forty seconds, and climbing at a predetermined uniform rate to the required altitude (where there had to be 1,500 feet vertical of clear air in which to manoeuvre), they formed up in the close-knit formations which were vital for high concentration bombing and for effective mutual defence.

After the bombing force had departed, there followed the ordeal of waiting until the planes were due back—a normal mission could last for eight to ten hours. If it was winter the daylight would be fading as those on the base strained for the first faint drone of the returning aircraft. Several formations making for other airfields might overfly before the "locals" approached the runway. Then the base lights would be switched on and the aircraft would put on their landing lights, and one by one they would peel off to land. As they broke formation and circled, on the ground the commanding officers of the squadrons tried to read identification numbers with field-glasses to see if everyone had returned.

Describing such a scene at Ridgewell, the chaplain wrote:

> We stood on the outside of the upper walk of the control tower, scanning the horizon. It was the ETA, the estimated time of arrival. We saw in the distance the tiny objects which we thought to be our planes. When they got close enough, we began to count. We had sent out twenty-one planes; only nineteen returned. The men's faces at my side turned a grayish color and showed signs of crying—but they kept back the tears. They were not prepared for this shock on our very first mission.[22]

If, after a raid, one plane came straight to the field ahead of the rest, or fired double red flares as it came in, that meant it had a wounded man or men aboard. It might also flash its lights and when the pilot had landed he might keep his flaps down, and if that happened an ambulance would rush to the plane as soon as it stopped.

Occasionally, pilots just failed to make it home and planes crashed near base. On 5th November a Fortress returning from an attack on Gelsenkirchen, in Germany, crossed the coast with only one engine still operating, its nose smashed, much of the horizontal stabiliser shot away, and its controls so badly damaged that it was considered impossible to make a safe landing. At 3,000 feet the twenty-three-year-old pilot ordered his crew to bail out, then set the plane on auto pilot on a

Other aircrew and ground staff look on anxiously as a wounded man is lifted gently from a B-17 Fortress and put into an ambulance.   *USAF*

"Blazing Heat" leads Martin B-26 Marauders of the 386th Bomb Group to the runway at Boxted, Essex, for a raid on France in August.   *Imperial War Museum*

course which would take it back out to sea. As he prepared to jump himself, he realised that the plane was in a downward glide that would take it to the centre of Ipswich so, placing his life at risk, he returned to the controls, pulled the Fortress out of its dive at 200 feet, turned it away from the town, cut the engine and crash-landed it on its belly in a field on the outskirts of the town.

Two weeks later a rather similar incident at Redlingfield, Suffolk, ended tragically. The plane caught fire, the bombs and ammunition on board exploded, and all the US aircrew were killed and two village families made homeless.

When things went well and everyone came back safely there was emotion of a different kind:

> The men grab one another around the shoulders and hug each other. They have not seen each other for eight hours. When they step out of the plane on their return, it is like a family reunion. Each is congratulating the other on coming back . . . When the doors of the plane are opened, the fellows greet each other with inexpressible joy . . .
>
> The crews assemble in the interrogation room. Here they jam the place, drinking their cup of cocoa and eating Spam sandwiches. The place is so full of men, one can hardly worm his way through. They are removing their heavy clothes, drinking cocoa, and reporting at the interrogation tables all at the same time and all amid chatter. This getting together is like manna from heaven. They never say "We knocked hell out of the enemy". Such words are never part of their conversation.[23]

Sometimes accidents brought the dangers right home to the base, as at Alconbury at 8.30 pm on 27th May, when as ground personnel were bombing up a B-17 Fortress one of the bombs detonated and set off several others. Nineteen men were killed and twenty-one injured; four B-17s were destroyed and eleven damaged. Two days later a B-26 Marauder crashed on to the airfield at Bury St Edmunds, killing the crew and damaging a hangar. On 23rd June, early in the morning, the entire base at Ridgewell was shaken by an explosion while preparations for a mission were in progress. No-one knew what happened; there were no survivors to tell the story, but thirteen of sixteen bombs which were being loaded into a Fortress exploded; the Fortress was obliterated and a second plane so badly damaged it had to be scrapped. Twenty-three men died. In another incident, at Great Ashfield on 3rd September, a bombed-up B-17 caught fire and exploded, badly damaging a hangar.

The British, too, suffered disasters. There was a dramatic episode at Chevington, near Bury St Edmunds, on 9th March when an RAF bomber carrying its full load of bombs crashed near Tan Office Farm. Police-constable Herbert G. Lander, of Wickhambrook, watched the plane come down, dashed across fields towards it, and found the main part of the fuselage, but the wreckage was strewn over a wide area, most of it burning, and he could not find the crew. The farmer, Mr Frederick E. Pettingale, who was on the other side of the meadow, found a number of survivors, all burned and injured. He signalled the policeman with a whistle; they tried to make the airmen comfortable, laying them on parachutes and Mae Wests. Ambulances could not reach the scene, so Mr Pettingale guided the ambulancemen across the fields and helped them carry the casualties on stretchers, all the time knowing that behind him the fire was threatening his own premises.

The whole area had to be evacuated because of the danger from the unexploded bombs scattered around the crash site, and the village hall and feeding centre was used as accommodation until next day an RAF bomb disposal squad moved in and made things safe.

In the run-up to Christmas on 16th December, No 97 squadron of Bomber Command at Bourn despatched twenty-one Lancasters for a raid on Berlin. When they returned, visibility was very bad over the airfield. Eight planes landed safely at Bourn and three others at Graveley; a twelfth, badly damaged, reached Downham Market, but the other nine crashed in the surrounding countryside and twenty-eight aircrew were killed. The following day, 17th December, thirteen men were killed when four Halifaxes crashed while trying to land in haze at an emergency airfield at Woodbridge. This emergency landing ground on Sutton Heath had been opened only a month earlier to receive damaged bombers limping home from Europe; it had been given a greatly enlarged landing strip, five times the normal width, which had involved clearing over a million small trees of a Forestry Commission plantation.

The year ended with Britain's prospects of victory greatly improved. The great bombing offensive had played a part in securing that improvement, but the cost in men and machines was immense, a foretaste of the sacrificial struggle that lay ahead.

CHAPTER THREE

Strangers in the Midst

THE PEOPLE of East Anglia. a region so long insulated from the outside world, had been suddenly engulfed by a mass of strangers, but by 1943 they were getting used to this enlargement of their world. First there had come the British Servicemen and women: soldiers to guard their coasts in the days when invasion was a daily possibility, airmen to fight the Battle of Britain from local airfields or to man the bomber bases, Navy personnel to commandeer the ports along the North Sea coast. East Anglians quickly got used to sharing their streets, their pubs, their dance halls and cinemas with these visitors. In the days after Dunkirk they made acquaintance, too, with men from distant lands: Canadians, Australians and New Zealanders serving at bomber bases, Free French sailors wearing striped shirts and red pompoms, Polish officers with hats like mortarboards, Dutch and Norwegian soldiers, Czech airmen, and a small number of Americans who had voluntarily crossed the Atlantic to fly with the RAF in so-called Eagle squadrons.

All were received in a spirit of goodwill, tinged with curiosity, and no serious problems arose. An Anglo-Polish Society took root in Suffolk, with the Earl of Stradbroke as its president; it organised cultural and social events in Ipswich and elsewhere. A Polish Army Choir performed at Cambridge Guildhall. A comparable Yugoslavia Society recruited fifty-eight members in Cambridge in its first year.

Social life was greatly enhanced for some local residents; for example, an Ipswich girl who cycled to four village dances every week. "All the villages ran at least one a week, and frequently more," she said. She recalled "endeavouring to stagger them from neighbourhood to neighbourhood . . . I danced with Czechs, Dutchmen, Scots, Americans, Poles, French and, of course, men from all over England, Wales and Ireland—and even a New Zealander . . ."[1]

For more than three years the East Anglian way of life had been under severe pressure, as local men were called to the Services and local women into the fields and factories. Now an influx of strangers brought bigger changes. Not all who arrived were fighting Allies. By the beginning of 1943 there were over eight thousand Italian prisoners-of-war in the eastern counties, housed in eleven camps, and 44,000 more arrived during the year.

The authorities ruled that there must be no fraternisation between these Italians and local residents, but this proved extremely difficult to impose, and up to a point the authorities turned a blind eye. There were frequent prosecutions, however, designed to discourage close relationships.

In May a thirty-four-year-old Barrow married woman, mother of three

Terence Dalton are publishers of high-quality non-fiction illustrated books on a variety of subjects, particularly maritime and aeronautical history, as well as general books of East Anglian interest.

If you would like to receive details of our other publications please complete this card and return it to us. No stamp required.

Name_____

Address:_____

_____ Postcode:_____

Special interests (please circle):

Maritime   Aviation

East Anglia   Rivers

Other (please state)_____

_____

2

Terence Dalton Limited,

47 Water Street,

Lavenham,

SUDBURY,

Suffolk.

CO10 8BR

children, was fined £1 at Bury St Edmunds for "fraternising with an Italian prisoner-of-war, thereby committing an act likely to prejudice discipline". She had been habitually speaking to one particular prisoner-of-war in a quiet place in the late evening, the prosecuting solicitor said. The woman told the court: "I would not have known the man if I had not worked on the same farm with him," adding "I have seen other people talking, and they are still talking."

In another case, at Great Bardfield, the defending solicitor asked a police witness: "Do you know that British people are talking with the Italian prisoners?" The detective replied: "Yes, they are, and we are trying to stamp it out." This was a case in which two land girls were brought before the court for "unlawfully despatching letters to two Italian prisoners-of-war at Finchingfield". They had been ditching on the same farm, and they wrote to the Italians because the prisoners had said they were lonely. The prosecution admitted that the letters were "purely personal" and contained nothing to endanger the security of the state, and therefore no suggestion of immorality.

Similarly, when three girls were brought before the Huntingdon court charged with sending letters to Italians "otherwise than by post", the prosecuting solicitor made a point of stating that nothing sinister was involved and there was no suggestion against the morals of any of the women. But he thought it was shocking that there should be conduct of this kind—"the national enemy is the private enemy, and these men with whom there were these intimate friendships are men whose purpose it has been to destroy everything these women enjoyed, and to kill

A parade of Dutch personnel working with RAF Coastal Command at Bircham Newton on 4th January.
Imperial War Museum

our own flesh and blood". The two girls who had written the letters were each fined £1; both were in the Women's Land Army, and one, although herself a British subject, had Italian-born parents and was able to speak Italian. The third girl had delivered the letters—she was daughter of the landlord of a public house where an Italian called daily—and she was fined ten shillings.

One of the most extraordinary cases was at Braintree. The evidence was that three Italian prisoners-of-war had been patients in the Essex County Hospital at Colchester for two months, at the same time as a Belgian soldier. When the Belgian was discharged from hospital he asked his wife to send a parcel of food and cigarettes to the Italians and she addressed it to the hospital ward nurse, requesting that she forward it. The Belgian soldier, his wife and the nurse were all charged and brought to court. The prosecuting solicitor said there was nothing sinister about the case; the three accused pleaded ignorance of the regulations and said their only intention had been to be kind to the prisoners. This case was dismissed on payment of costs.

Despite the official attitude, there was little ill-feeling towards the Italians, and their ready smiles and relaxed attitudes earned them a good deal of sympathy. One Sunday in April one of them, twenty-nine-year-old Surgeon Lieutenant Mario Luchi, of the Royal Italian Navy, who before the war had represented Padua University as a swimmer, risked his life to save a six-year-old boy from drowning in the River Cam. A suggestion was made publicly that it would be an appropriate British gesture to offer to repatriate him, if he wanted to go. Instead he received a Royal Humane Society parchment from the hands of the Mayor of Cambridge.

Absorbing the Americans proved more difficult. Early arrivals were greeted with considerable interest, usually with a benevolent reticence, but in some places with enthusiasm. Robert Arbib, an engineer who arrived at the end of 1942 to help construct a new airfield at Debach, in Suffolk, described how he and half a dozen colleagues made their first acquaintance with the locals at the Grundisburgh inn, The Dog:

> Someone must have seen us go into The Dog, for soon the villagers began to arrive. By ones or twos they came, and sat themselves down in their accustomed seats . . . This Saturday evening there was excitement and a high tempo in every room in The Dog.
> "The Yanks have arrived. There are seven of them in The Dog right now." People came in from all the farms and cottages and they filled the old public house with a carnival spirit. By eight o'clock there was standing room only . . .
> "The Yanks have arrived. The work on our aerodrome is about to begin at last. It has begun already!" . . . The last round we bought was for 47 drinks . . . The word Yanks was on everyone's lips . . . On the following Tuesday The Dog went dry and closed—for the first time in 450 years.[(2)]

When a new group arrived in East Anglia, the men were usually confined to their base for the first month. At most of the bases there were American Red Cross Clubs, where dances were regularly arranged. Some bases had professional bands, like the 447th Heavy Bombardment Group at Rattlesden, whose "Blockbusters" orchestra was composed of musicians drafted into the US Army Air Force; it played at many venues, including Ipswich Cornhill. Other bases formed bands with whatever talent they could find among their enlisted personnel. Local girls were invited to the dances, which opened up a new world to them. It was not, one of them reported, "the correct ballroom dancing we had learned at school. It was a slow cheek-to-cheek shuffle, to the music of Tommy Dorsey and Artie Shaw, or an exciting jitterbug". *The* music that swept all before it was that of Glenn Miller—such tunes as *Chattanooga Choo-choo*, *Little Brown Jug*, *Moonlight Serenade* and *Tuxedo Junction*. His Big Band played in hangars all over East Anglia. The licensee of one Norwich pub was performing at the piano when an unknown American remarked: "You're playing that tune all wrong." Annoyed, she suggested he might like to show whether he could do better. He sat down and played brilliantly, then revealed that he was Glenn Miller[3].

The British had something to offer in return, teaching the Americans *Chestnut Tree*, the *Valeta*, and the *Boston Two-Step*, English dances new to them.

There were also film shows in the base cinemas and live shows in the canteens. Local entertainers were often engaged—Madame Osina's Children's Dancing Troupe from Norwich was a particular favourite—but sometimes there would be a ripple of excitement when local residents caught a glimpse of a famous American face, for Hollywood stars occasionally came to visit. Several local lasses had the pleasure of dancing with film star James Stewart during the time he served as Captain Stewart, group executive officer at Tibenham, Hardwick and Old Buckenham.

After their first month at a base in Britain 15 per cent of personnel were allowed out at one time, which meant leave once a week. The American Red Cross opened clubs and canteens in all the main towns, but these could cater for only a fraction of the men, and most of them went to the local cinemas, dance halls, and pubs. In Norwich there were weekly basketball sessions and boxing bouts in Blackfriars Hall, and occasional baseball games at Carrow Road.

What made the American invasion different from anything that had gone before were the numbers involved. Towns as big as Ipswich could be swamped. When the liberty trucks left the camps at 7 pm every one was packed with far more than the fourteen men for whom there were seats beneath the low tarpaulin hoods. When they returned from the towns at 11 pm the collection points, the Cattle Market in Norwich, Princes Street in Ipswich and the Drummer Street bus station in Cambridge, were chaotic, with several hundred men trying to find their trucks. The Mass Observation organisation sent an investigator to Peterborough and he reported that:

> In the evening the streets are crowded with Americans, and it seemed to me very few other people . . . The town almost gives the impression of one that has been "occupied" in Europe. The Peterborough people seem suspicious and unfriendly, and keep themselves to themselves.[4]

This same organisation endeavoured to get a broad impression of public attitudes to the American servicemen early in 1943, and came up with a formula that 48 per cent of the people they questioned were pro-American, 22 per cent were anti-American and 30 per cent were neutral. The things people liked about the Americans were their friendliness, generosity, frankness and kindness. The thing they disliked was their boastfulness. This January survey of British feeling about America and the Americans indicated some possible areas of misunderstanding:

> Americans are not used to the easy English habits of casual acquaintanceships with girls. Whereas in England it is possible to pick up a girl in the street or in a dance hall and for her to be entirely respectable, the American finds it difficult to treat her as otherwise than "cheap". Also, the American idiom is different. When he says "Are you going to take me home?" to the girl he has just met, he means "home, to sit on your porch and meet your folks", but English girls feel insulted by the suggestion, which to them has a different meaning.[5]

Despite such misunderstandings, Americans quickly made a hit with most young women. The open way in which they voiced compliments about their appearance ("You look swell"), the way they offered a girl a chair to sit down or jumped up when she first entered a room or left a group to visit the powder room,

Many British families provided a home-from-home for American servicemen. Here the Garrard family at Great Glemham enjoy a game of cards with two off-duty airmen from the nearby Framlingham air base. *Mrs Faith Garrard*

the manner in which they helped their companion take their coats from their shoulders in cinemas, these were courtesies that many English girls had not enjoyed before. And, when friendships had been established, the Americans were generous with presents. "We felt like queens," one girl declared.

American generosity manifested itself in many ways, and some of the men seem to have been affected by the contrast between their earnings and those of the East Anglians.

When the Linton magistrates dismissed a case against a British private in the Pioneer Corps accused of having been drunk and incapable on the highway, they ordered him to pay nineteen shillings court costs. He told the court he was paid twenty-one shillings a week in the Army and he had a large family and a wife with tuberculosis. His sergeant said that he had done very well at Dunkirk, and his commanding officer wrote praising his character in the Army. An American sergeant who was in court, but who had never set eyes on the man before, came forward and paid the nineteen shillings, remarking afterwards: "I didn't like to see a guy like that get into trouble."

A Cambridge diarist wrote in March of a US soldier to whom he had chatted that:

> He was disgusted by the poverty in England. He had talked to several workmen and been horrified at their low wages.[6]

At about the same time a Bury St Edmunds diarist, Miss Winifred Last, wrote:

> USA soldiers seem to like giving sweets to children. One of them offered to pay for my late landlady's greengrocery as she purchased from a cart at the door, and on her refusal followed the cart and paid for another householder's. Perhaps some of them realise our native poverty . . .[7]

Most of the Americans were also good with children, as one English lady who worked in canteens remarked:

> Tough, gum-chewing, girl-chasing, hard-drinking GIs—let one small child cross his path and he is lost; your Yank is always a sucker for kids.[8]

They were also soft-hearted about pets, some of which were unusual—when the 390th Bomb Group came to Framlingham in July they brought a honey bear, which occasionally escaped into the nearby countryside. Dogs "orphaned" when their owners were shot down on flying missions became a problem when they were left to roam, and farmers lost poultry and sheep.

Many Americans exhibited a serious turn of mind. Some were ardent churchgoers:

> Worshippers from Alabama to Utah found the Baptist and Methodist churches of Dereham, and found a welcome and a friendship that was to last. There they met, and worshipped, and joined in the meetings of the Christian Endeavour group on Wednesday evenings . . . One of the "boys" played the accordion—another the piano—and all of them together made a rousing choir.[9]

In Swanton Novers, near Melton Constable, Americans met the cost of a coach that went round the villages and outlying farms to take worshippers to the Salvation Army's Friday evening meetings in Fakenham.

Americans visited Cambridge in large and ever-increasing numbers: not only men from the nearby bases, but others intent on sightseeing in the old university town. A few attended special academic courses (at Oxford as well as Cambridge); one of the earliest of these was at Emmanuel College, Cambridge, in June, 1943. In that month the Cambridge American Hospitality Committee reported that, on an average day, 244 soldiers reserved a bed (or a chair, or a portion of floor) for the night, 578 main meals were served, and 553 snacks. Over 160 English ladies were on the rota, most of them unpaid volunteers. By that time the Bull Hotel had been formally handed over to the US Red Cross for use as a leave centre; earlier overnight accommodation for visiting Servicemen had been in the lecture hall in St Andrews Street, in the Baptist Church, in guest rooms in some of the colleges, or in private homes.

Norwich also attracted many sightseers from the American bases. The Bishop's Palace was made available to the American Red Cross, and officially opened on 10th May, when the Bishop handed over a key. The *Eastern Daily Press* reported:

> They have equipped many rooms as dormitories, installed dozens of showers, which Americans prefer to baths, and transformed the ancient vaulted kitchens with rows of modern cooking and refrigerating apparatus. One room of the Palace has become a modern cafeteria. Any morning one may find the Bishop of Norwich there, drinking coffee with men on leave or posing for snapshots in groups that are reaching scores of American homes—a guest in his own Palace almost, save that he has retained his library for personal use.

Another house in The Close was also taken over and equipped with two-tier bunks; even so, it was impossible to meet the demand. A full entertainment programme was organised, with outings to the Broads, tennis competitions on the lawns of local friends, Sunday garden parties in the Palace grounds, and weekday entertainments for which stage and screen artists travelled from the US, receiving only expenses.

Anglo-American Services Clubs opened in all the smaller towns that were much visited by US Servicemen and women. With big gestures and small, everything was done to spread understanding and goodwill. The Syndics of the Cambridge University Press gave £44,000 to endow a chair of American History and Institutions, and Professor James Dobie came from Texas University, took up residence in Emmanuel and gave his first lecture in October. In that month, too, a group of American officers stationed at Knettishall donated a plaque in memory of Tom Paine, one of the most distinguished (if controversial) sons of Thetford, the author of *The Rights of Man*, who, going to Pennsylvania in 1774, immediately began campaigning for freedom for the slaves. He was credited with being the first

Professor Frank Dobie, a Cambridge history don, talking to one of the crew of a B-17 Fortress named after Tom Paine, author of *The Rights of Man*, during a visit to Knettishall. *Imperial War Museum*

man to use the term "United States of America". At Knettishall an Eighth USAAF plane was named "Tom Paine" and carried his quotation: "Tyranny, like hell, is not easily conquered."

As these various activities gathered momentum, many good Anglo-American friendships were formed, some of which blossomed into romance. At most weddings at this time the grooms, and often the brides as well, were in uniform, and every month some of the uniforms were American or Canadian. The *Cambridge Daily News* published two photographs in January of local girls marrying Canadian airmen. In mid-February another photograph of a staff sergeant from Wyoming and his Cambridge bride was stated to be the sixth wedding in which a member of the US forces had been married at the Cambridge Register Office on Castle Hill. After that, there was a regular stream of such weddings. The first in Bury St Edmunds was at St Mary's on 27th February, when Staff Sergeant Stanley Edward

Many Americans soon made friends with the "natives". Here an American airman poses with his fiancée and friends outside Church Farm, Great Glemham.   *Mrs Faith Garrard*

Maspens, of Cincinnatti, Ohio, married Miss Teresa Ella Baldwin, of Churchgate Street, Bury, whose father was chairman of the local British Legion Club. At the end of the year Norwich witnessed the first wedding of an Englishman to a member of the US women's forces: Mr Thomas Thompson, grandson of a one-time MP for Great Yarmouth, Sir Arthur Harbord, married Sergeant Jane Freytag, of the American WAC.

Many American lads, however, looked for a substitute "mom" rather than a bride. They longed for an invitation to a British home, and local Anglo-American hospitality committees were created, under the auspices of the American Red Cross, to arrange such visits, usually for a single meal, but sometimes for a man's whole leave period*. In many places—Wendling was one—there was a "Mother for a Day" scheme under which arrangements were made for a British woman to "adopt" a lonely GI, going to lunch in a Red Cross club as his guest and then taking him home for tea.

*Between November, 1943, and the end of the war they arranged one and a quarter million such visits.

44

There were, nonetheless, many English with anti-American views, and there were many Americans whose behaviour fed such prejudices. Norwich produced a good example of sensitivity lacking on both sides. A local entrepreneur salvaged a few open landaus from a city stable, harnessed a pair of horses to each, and planned to make a quick buck hiring them out. Many GIs were happy to see the local sights in this manner but, riding high above citizens who were less affluent, less well-fed and less relaxed, cigar-smoking Americans were not an endearing spectacle. Nevertheless, when one of the landau drivers charged his passengers fifty shillings, when the correct fare was only six shillings, he received little sympathy and was fined £2. The Chief Constable, who said there was much similar behaviour in the city, warned that he intended to prosecute in every case, and the *Eastern Daily Press* published a leader supporting the idea of severe penalties:

> It is generally weeks before the American in England can know with confidence whether he is getting his right change when he buys anything, or what coins he should tender when making a payment. In many cases all he can do is to hold out an assortment of coins and trust to the honesty of the shopkeeper. . . . We have heard numbers of complaints about Americans being overcharged.

William Stock, the Chelmsford diarist already quoted, had taken a job in a local hospital and at the end of April he noted:

> Some men at lunchtime were talking about American troops in this country and all agreed that they were untidy, slack, spoke a different language, were altogether different from us. This seems a pretty widespread opinion.[10]

Another diarist, Mrs Sarah Williams, travelled from Sheringham to visit ex-colleagues in her old haunts in Norwich, and afterwards she wrote:

> The whole place looks scruffy. It's the Americans. I went into a restaurant which before the war was all right and it was nauseating. It was dirty and the food was appalling, and the prices exorbitant. There were several Americans with girls and they were all drunk to the point of vomit. Sister — says she often sees whole groups quite drunk at two, holding each other up, and she never goes into any restaurant unless the same thing happens. And many girls just fling themselves into the Americans' arms, because they have so much money. After talking to several people, I have a feeling that there will be very little Anglo-American friendship left.[11]

It is interesting to set this impression beside that of an equally sensitive American, Robert Arbib, who wrote this description of Ipswich at much the same time:

> It was a dirty, smelly, crowded old town after dark, this Ipswich of the war. Little streams of urine ran down from doorways into the gutter, and in some doorways there were the dark forms of a boy and a girl pressed close together. The night air had a musty, old, stale smell: the smell of fried fish, of coal smoke, of horse manure and of fog, and the sea. It smelled of beer and rain and aged, mouldy stones. The flat-paned windows were gaping and vacant, the streets narrow, cobble-stoned and dark. It was not until midnight that they became silent and empty and you could hear again the echo of your own footsteps, and far down by the River Orwell the clanking and screaming of the trains.[12]

The wisest observers tried to keep things in perspective, as, for example, Jean Lancaster-Rennie, who from January, 1943, was employed as second chef at the American Officers' Club in Bethel Street, Norwich:

They were not all angels. A mixed bag from a nation of around 200,000,000 people couldn't possibly be all the same. Some of the boys *did* boast openly about the money they earned. Some silly girls *did* have their heads turned . . .[13]

A Norwich diarist, a lecturer at the Training College, also showed a proper sense of balance:

Roosevelt is fine. The Americans here are a mixed lot and a few can destroy the reputations of many. I hope we shall get to understand one another better.[14]

In August, 1943, the Mass Observation organisation did another survey of opinion in Peterborough, and its investigator concluded that there was great resentment of the American troops stationed locally.[15]

Members of the Garrard family have a close look at a 390th Bomb Group B-17 at Framlingham. Baby Rockford is perched on no 3 engine under the watchful eye of the crew chief. *Mrs Faith Garrard*

This investigator added:

> The city has been inundated with American airmen, who are stationed a short way out of the city. In the evening the streets are crowded with Americans, and it seemed to me very few other people. There are the usual stories of drinking with young girls in pubs, "goings-on" in air raid shelters, and so forth . . .

A large number of the Americans in East Anglia, particularly those in the engineer battalions which came to construct new airfields, were black. News of their presence was allowed to filter out only slowly[16], because both American and British governments exhibited a consciousness of colour prejudice which, as events proved, did not reflect the attitude of the ordinary people of Britain. *They* received the visitors in a natural and friendly way; sometimes, it seemed, they "took to" the black Americans better than to their white colleagues. They may have been influenced by the fact that about 10,000 West Indians had already been smoothly integrated into the RAF, or, more probably, they may simply have preferred the humility of most of the blacks to the boastfulness of some of the whites. In Ipswich a Women's Voluntary Service member who helped in the local YMCA found that she had to *persuade* the American blacks that "they were allowed to walk on the pavement when white people were on there, too, that they could use the trolley-buses, go into restaurants, shops, etc"[17].

An observer for the Mass Observation organisation noted:

> The Negro's approach to the white girl is entirely different. He is awed and flattered that she should speak to him at all. All he wants is the honour and glory of actually having a white girl for his friend. He gets the same generous pay as the white soldier* and he is prepared to spend it all on the girl, and quite often expect nothing in return save her company.[18]

The British War Cabinet, after long deliberation, agreed on 13th October, 1942, that "it was desirable that the people of this country should avoid becoming too friendly with coloured American troops", but that Americans "must not expect our authorities, civil or military, to assist them in enforcing a policy of segregation". Above all, the Cabinet was anxious that there should be no public discussion of the subject. The War Office issued guidance to the effect that British residents should "remember that they [black Americans] are not accustomed in their own country to close and intimate relationships with white people . . . For a white woman to go about in the company of a Negro American is likely to lead to controversy and ill-feeling."

The US Army, at this stage of the war, was not prepared to use blacks as fighting troops†, but only in what had been their traditional roles since the Civil War, as construction and maintenance labourers, truck drivers, storemen and

---

*£15 per month.
†This policy was changed towards the end of 1944.

ordnance workers. The Americans also made extensive use of "zoning", under which certain towns or villages or individual public houses were reserved for the use of one racial group or the other. Thus, Rougham was placed off limits to whites, while the licensee of the Duke of York at Ditchingham, near Bungay, accepted the suggestion of the local Provost Marshal that his pub, serving Seething and Flixton airfields and a bomb dump at Earsham, should be for blacks only.

In September, 1943, Colonel (later Brigadier-General) Oliver Haines, of the Inspector General's Department of the US Army, arrived in Europe to look into these and other matters, and he began his inspections in East Anglia. In his first report, dated Ipswich, 21st November, he wrote:

> Blacks were stationed at Eye, at Debach, near Ipswich, and in Haughley Park, near Stowmarket, where they were particularly popular with the locals because of their swing bands and dances. The white troops were in different towns—Martlesham, Wattisham and Horham. For both races the night life was in Ipswich, with its 150 public houses. There being more white than black troops, their commanders decided that the whites should have access to the majority of places of entertainment, and so just eight pubs, a Co-op dance hall and a Red Cross Club were "reserved" for blacks alone.
>
> In the larger area, local officers determined that the ironically named River Dove, a tributary of the Waveney, was to be the border line. Eye and Diss were "black" towns, but all the villages east of the Dove were "out of bounds" for the blacks . . . Eye, being just on the river, was a "black" town, while Horham, four miles away, was "white". Evidence that segregation was strictly adhered to was provided by the frequent arrests of blacks found in areas out of bounds to them.
>
> If, as often happened in remote parts of Britain, troops were based in places where opportunities for recreation were few, then rotation of pass days allowed them to be shared—"blacks Tuesdays, whites Wednesday".[19]

In a later report, dated 3rd December, Colonel Haines dealt with one particular case where a complaint was made against black Americans in general:

> In Norfolk, Mrs Carr, wife of Brigadier Carr, the owner of Ditchingham Hall, sent her complaints about black GIs to Lord Cecil, who passed them on to the American authorities. . . . Mrs Carr didn't like blacks in the Hall. She was upset that the blacks attracted women and, according to her, sent trucks into town to collect them. An American investigation showed that the allegations were unfounded, a view echoed by the caretaker's wife. She said simply that she found the black GIs "very well behaved . . . no trouble to us". Her little girl had cried when they left and in her opinion there had been greater numbers of camp followers around when British troops were based in the area.[20]

The only serious evidence of racial tension occurred *within* the US Services. According to one survey, there was an average of four violent clashes a week between white and black Americans, the majority of which occurred in the south and south-west of England—at Winchester there were three in a single day.[21]

Prejudice was very much alive, however, on the East Anglian bases. The Ipswich WVS lady who has been quoted above attended a New Year's dance at the coloured American base at Eye. Her party was driven there in trucks and the function took place under what may be described as "controlled conditions". No alcohol was permitted, only soft drinks and coffee, and white Military Policemen stood around the hall, watching. A jazz band played throughout the evening, the food was delicious, and everything went with a swing . . . until, at midnight, the girls went back to the lorries to go home, and some of the blacks came outside to say goodnight. According to this woman's testimony, "the MPs beat the boys who came out unmercifully, so that any pleasure we may have had at the party was spoilt for us all".[22]

A young Suffolk girl who worked in the canteen at Great Ashfield related a more horrifying experience:

> When the GIs on our base had nothing better to do, they got together in bands of 12 or even 20, armed themselves to the teeth with razors, cut-throats, and knives and would then go off on what they called nigger-hunting. . . . We were appalled at it and said so. . . . The white American authorities turned a completely blind eye to it, in fact when we talked to the CO we were told to mind our goddam business . . .[23]

Only very rarely was there a *fracas* involving Americans and locals. In one such four Suffolk men described as "van dwellers of the gypsy type" were involved in a pub brawl at Ixworth Thorpe, when they shouted "We don't want you Yanks over here." One of the Americans replied: "Our officer has given us instructions not to fight with anyone over here," but fists were raised and bottles thrown, and the four local men appeared at West Suffolk Quarter Sessions and were sent to prison.

If Americans offended and came into the hands of the British police they were handed over to the US authorities for punishment, and American courts-martial took place regularly in the Guildhall at Cambridge, and some in Ipswich. Sentences were severe. The usual charges involved violence in some form.

In January a black US soldier was sentenced to death when he was found guilty of shooting and killing an officer at his camp. In May another was found guilty of "voluntary manslaughter" of a thirty-five-year-old Diss garage assistant and sentenced to ten years' hard labour and dishonourable discharge; the victim, according to the evidence, had made an "indecent approach" not only to the American defendant but to others as well. Just before Christmas the Essex CID handed over to the American military authorities two black US soldiers who had been detained following the death of a twenty-eight-year-old Colchester taxi driver, whose strangled body was found in the grounds of Birch Rectory.

Some charges concerned assaults on women. In March a twenty-four-year-old private, who had no previous convictions, was found guilty of a criminal assault on a young woman at Tiptree and sentenced to hard labour for life, dishonourable discharge, and forfeiture of all rights and property.

In May two black Americans were sentenced to five years' hard labour and dishonourable discharge when found guilty of attempted rape and of robbery or theft. The woman in one of these cases, who was nineteen and whom the defendant

EAST ANGLIAN DAILY TIMES,   THURSDA

HIS FORFEIT—A MOCK PROPOSAL: During a round game at a party organised for American boys, Sergt. Benny Dalewske, Chicago, failed to catch the spinning plate and had to pay a forfeit. Here he is doing it—making a mock proposal to the girl of his choice. But she was already married, being Mrs. M. M. Perry, of Stowmarket. The party took place at one of the three Anglo-American Y.M.C.A. clubs recently opened in this country. As well as providing refreshments, reading, writing and games rooms, the clubs supply a common meeting-place for British and American Service men. (Photo. Current Affairs.)

Anglo-American clubs run by the YMCA and other bodies provided meeting places for both British and American servicemen. During a party at one of them a young American sergeant had to pay a forfeit—making a mock proposal to a Stowmarket woman, who, it seems, was already married.   *East Anglian Daily Times*

had met in a public house in Eye, was known to the police; an inspector told the court that she had been only sixteen when "he first had to speak to her with regard to her frequenting public houses".

There was a procession of other servicemen, American and British, before the courts during the year, but only those with preconceived prejudice would have discerned racial overtones in the patterns of misbehaviour.

To help keep things in perspective, an Ipswich reader of the *East Anglian Daily Times* suggested that black American troops might give a concert of Negro spirituals in Ipswich. "Apart from the delight of hearing them sing, it would, I feel sure, give these strangers a feeling of our friendliness towards them," this correspondent wrote. The idea was taken up, and a US Army Negro Chorus of two hundred, drawn from aviation engineering battalions, performed at Ipswich Public Hall on 25th November, under the auspices of the American Red Cross. The hall was packed to overflowing; an anonymous correspondent had written to the *East Anglian Daily Times* a few days before:

I trust that should this be read by any who have hitherto had an unkind, criticising attitude towards these people, they will decide to listen to the concert, after which their view must surely turn to friendliness.

Exceptional efforts were made at Christmas to generate additional goodwill.

The scale of some of the parties almost overwhelmed the participants. At Ridgewell the American chaplain, the Reverend James Good Brown, visited schools in all the villages surrounding the base to invite their pupils to a party. He checked that there were 263 children on roll in these schools, so the Americans prepared a party for 250.

> When Santa Claus began to give out gifts at the party, he gave to 375 children—more than 100 above our estimate. Where the children came from, God only knows! The children were at the schools waiting when the trucks arrived. They came from some places, from villages, beyond the area of schools which I had visited. Furthermore they had with them the little tots, brothers and sisters below school age. The truck drivers from our base were astounded. I had told them how many children would be at a certain school. There were twice that number.[24]

So, when it came to giving out the presents from Santa, there weren't enough. The hosts collected up all the games which had been sent over for the GIs' leisure, and men went to their barracks and brought out gifts they had been sent by their families. They managed to find just enough. No effort was spared to make this a great party:

> A staff sergeant constructed a large Santa which was suspended from high wires over the base. A large sleigh was made for Santa, who sat proudly driving his reindeer. Each reindeer was constructed of wood and was six to eight feet high. These were hitched to the sleigh and were headed towards the sky. The whole creation, Santa, sleigh and reindeer, was fully lighted with bright spotlights and could be seen from all over the aerodrome. It gave a festive atmosphere to Ridgewell Aerodrome.[25]

With great effort, the Americans presented a brave and friendly face to the outside world, but another diary presents a different picture of Ridgewell at Christmas, 1943:

> Mostly that day we sat around the little stove, drank ale and listened to Christmas music on the radio. And, of course, talked about the raids. We could never stay off of that subject very long. . . . Christmas Day 1943 was the most somber one I can remember. Mostly the men were withdrawn, lost in memories of happier times.[26]

At Honington, a hundred children from an orphans' home evacuated to Euston were invited to a party where they lined up to greet Santa Claus arriving "from America" in a Fortress, and then went to the Red Cross Club, a big Nissen hut decked with pine boughs, streamers, balloons, lanterns, and a fully-laden Christmas tree. There were lighted candles on the tables for dinner, and a menu which included such exotic and unheard-of dishes as roast pheasant with Yankee dressing and Southern giblet gravy, snowflake potatoes, buttered string beans, candied carrots, creamed corn, olives, hot biscuits, ice cream sundaes, cookies, and candy.

This party went on from 10 am to 4.30 pm. The station orchestra played and a choir sang carols, the children joining in. Entertainment included an accordion, a trick violinist and tap dancing. A highlight was the appearance of "a real live

English duke"—Honington was part of the estate of the Duke of Grafton, who was among the visitors.

Similar celebrations were organised by all the American bases. At Newmarket the USAAF was host to a group of thirty orphans from a nearby Dr Barnardo's home. At Bury St Edmunds the American Red Cross held a dance at the Co-op Hall for Americans and their girl friends and also, in co-operation with American engineers, played host to seven hundred children who packed the Corn Exchange for an afternoon of riotous entertainment. Later, on Christmas morning, about a hundred hampers of cakes, chocolates, candy and food were distributed to poor homes in the town, selected by the Mayor's committee. At Colchester the military police entertained ninety children whose fathers were prisoners-of-war.

A total of 1,100 children from Ipswich and surrounding villages were entertained at a country mansion "somewhere in East Anglia", including sixty in the care of the town's Social Welfare Committee. "It was difficult to say who

A practice bombing mission for the 388th Bomb Group from Knettishall over the Tollesbury range. Tollesbury pier can be seen just below B-17F "Slightly Dangerous II", which led the 388th on the Münster raid. *William Goldenberg*

A champagne reception for Lieutenant Paul Pennock on completion of his first tour of 25 missions as a pilot with the 379th Bomb Group at Kimbolton on 29th November. *USAF*

enjoyed themselves the most, the children or the Americans, each soldier having attached himself to one or two of the children, who became very great friends," reported the *East Anglian Daily Times*.

Not every effort at Anglo-American amity entirely succeeded. At Ridgewell the Reverend James Brown sought to stage a Christmas Festival of Music, with a mixed chorus composed of men from the base and ladies from the nearby villages; after trying a few rehearsals, he had to call off the event because not enough men on the base turned up. The ladies appeared willingly, riding through the night on their bikes; "they had to be placated," the chaplain noted in his diary.

Happily, there was much reciprocal entertainment, although it could not be on such a lavish scale. In all the eastern counties families invited servicemen into their homes. The Bury St Edmunds Anglo-American Committee arranged for about two hundred Americans to be invited in that area.

When 1943 had run its course, it was clear that such anti-American sentiment as had developed was primarily attributable to the "swamping" effect on local communities of so many GIs. Sensitive Americans well understood the problem. One of them, Robert Arbib, visited Sudbury late in the year, by which time there were four airfields and an American hospital within easy reach of the town—15,000 to 20,000 men—and he wrote:

American soldiers were everywhere—on the street corners, in the public houses—in countless aeroplanes overhead; and in trucks and jeeps on the streets. I heard a comment here and there: every American pilot seemed to have a girl in Sudbury, and showed his affection once a day by "buzzing" the town; the public houses were closing earlier and more often.[27]

With so many thousands of men on the bases, with a good deal of leisure time and limited recreational facilities to occupy them, there were large numbers who simply walked the streets. And on the streets many of the local girls strolled in pairs. Robert Arbib noted his impressions:

> Perhaps the chief attraction of Ipswich was the girls. It seemed to us then a town of girls, with a high proportion of young and pretty ones, and their behaviour was nothing like that of girls we had known at home. In the evening they walked along the pavements in pairs, smiling, swinging their supple hips in short skirts, looking after the soldiers, whispering "Hi, Yank", or whistling a phrase from *Yankee Doodle*.
>
> Many were young—14, 15 or 16, though we could not judge how old they were and they always said they were 18 at least. They had beautiful flowing hair, they wore tight sweaters and flat-heeled shoes, and they spoke that sing-song Suffolk dialect that often we could not fathom. They went unescorted to the dance halls and to the public houses and it was there that we met them.[28]

In this climate many older women came to feel threatened. A forty-seven-year-old Bury St Edmunds spinster, Winifred Last, confided to her diary:

> An American saw me home tonight from the centre of the town. Had a white face but Negroid characteristics. At the door wanted to kiss me and come in, but I rang for Mrs N— and told him someone was coming to the door, and so he made off. Perhaps he thought it might be my husband! I told him he was stupid walking about and trying to kiss strange women. Called me "darling" and when I objected said I must be somebody's darling, which I denied, quite truthfully. Kept trying to take my arm and put his arm round my waist as we walked. Bright moonlight night . . .[29]

Some Americans fully understood the problem that was building up and felt anxious, too:

> Many of us, and certainly many people of Ipswich, were disturbed by what they saw and heard, and by the easy familiarity of the young girls that roamed the streets and frequented the public houses. We had many a long and serious discussion on this topic. . . . Was it happening at home in our own land, in our own home town? We hoped that it wasn't, but we feared in our hearts that it was.[30]

CHAPTER FOUR

Menfolk Far Away

WHILE MEN from all over the world took up temporary quarters in East Anglia, husbands and fathers had been plucked from their homes in the region and scattered afar. Men serving in the county regiments fell into four groups during 1943: those in captivity in the Far East, those in India waiting for the time when an offensive could be mounted against the Japanese, those posted from Britain to the Mediterranean theatre, and those who were undergoing intensive training in the UK in preparation for the forthcoming invasion of Europe.

As 1943 opened the Japanese were being forced on to the defensive. They were in occupation of all the islands in the western and south-western area of the Pacific and the adjoining countries in South East Asia, and they had come dangerously close to the approaches to Australia. The first half of 1943 was a period of stalemate while the Americans, who had earlier begun to inflict heavy naval and air losses, prepared to counter-attack. Their first objective was to recapture a string of islands, culminating in the recapture of Rabaul, the main Japanese base, in New Britain. The Allies had agreed that this was a task primarily for the Americans, with assistance from the Australians, and it was midsummer before the offensive could begin.

Meanwhile, the survivors of three battalions of the Royal Norfolk Regiment, the 4th, 5th and 6th, two battalions of the Suffolk Regiment, the 4th and 5th, and the 1st and 2nd battalions of the Cambridgeshire Regiment were prisoners-of-war in Japanese hands. They had sailed from the Clyde towards the end of 1941 as part of the 18th Infantry Division and had arrived in Singapore as the last British troops were evacuating Malaya. After seventeen days of fighting, the remnants of these battalions were taken prisoner when Singapore surrendered.

Most of them remained for a large part of 1942 on Singapore Island, under conditions which were hard but tolerable. The British officers restored a fair measure of military discipline, and there was a full programme of drill parades, physical training, sports and education classes (up to university standard), with regular Sunday night concerts and occasional theatrical productions. The Japanese work regime was harsh; it required them to clear war damage and carry out reconstruction and to work in the docks. During this period six British soldiers who tried to escape were shot, and three British officers were compelled to witness their execution. The climate and the poor diet, which resulted in vitamin deficiencies, brought serious health problems: dysentery, malaria, tropical ulcers, skin complaints, and corneal ulcers of the eyes.

Back in East Anglia, the families of these men waited throughout 1942 with no

IPSWICH: Sir Richard Howard Vyse, chairman of Prisoners of War Department of the British Red Cross, photographed with workers at the Prisoners of War Depot in the Buttermarket on the occasion of his visit to Ipswich on Tuesday to launch the Suffolk £50,000 appeal for war prisoners. (E.A.D.T.)

The chairman of the British Red Cross Society's prisoners of war department, Sir Richard Howard Vyse, was photographed with workers at an Ipswich prisoners of war depot when he launched a £50,000 appeal in June. *East Anglian Daily Times*

reliable news of their fate. A statement from the War Office early in the New Year did little to relieve their anxiety:

> The majority of United Kingdom and Australian prisoners-of-war are still in camps in Malaya, Siam and Indo-China. No visits by the Red Cross or by the Protecting Power have been permitted. Work in these areas is understood to be very severe. Rations appear to be just sufficient to maintain health.

The first substantial list of prisoners came through from Japan in March, and regional newspapers then began regularly to publish short lists of names, but rarely more than a dozen at a time. When Lord Belstead visited Red Cross headquarters in London in March on behalf of the relatives he was told that the lists received from Tokyo contained barely one in ten of the names of those who had been posted missing, and most of those listed were officers. In a letter published in the *East Anglian Daily Times* he explained the communication difficulties. If there was a query about a name, it took the Red Cross two months to obtain clarification; letters sent by the prisoners-of-war might take six months or more to come through; letters addressed to them must be typed or most clearly written in block letters.

He was able to offer little comfort, but he strongly recommended next-of-kin to go on writing, even if they received no replies; and he added that his wife had arranged to have all their letters typewritten and posted if they were sent through her. The honorary secretary of the Cambridgeshire Troops Comforts Fund, Mrs Rawdon Briggs, also visited various offices in London in search of information about local men and then reported, through the local press:

> Without doubt, every possible effort . . . is being made. No one should give up hope, no matter how long the delay, or if your neighbour has heard and you have not. I have seen some of the photographic copies of the lists as sent by Japan. I have learnt that some 4,000 names have been received and I have had to realise by the evidence of my own eyes that no-one on earth could decipher or identify a large percentage of the names on these lists.

The same issue of the *Cambridge Daily News* published "the second list received from the headquarters of the British Red Cross and St John"; it contained only eight names.

Meanwhile, in Singapore the prisoners-of-war, including those from the East Anglian regiments, had been split up and scattered to Thailand, Burma, Indo-China, Formosa, the Philippines and Japan. The worst fate befell those who were sent to Thailand to construct a new metre-gauge railway, through virgin jungle and over mountains, to link Bangkok with Moulmein in Burma*. Both countries were now occupied by the Japanese. Altogether, 61,000 prisoners-of-war were employed on this project—not only British but also Dutch, Australian and American—and there was an enormous number of Chinese, Burmese and Tamil labourers.

The first parties of prisoners-of-war, which included men of the 2nd Battalion of the Cambridgeshire Regiment, left Singapore in mid-September, 1942, and others followed at intervals. The 4th and 5th Suffolks left by train early in November, and the Royal Norfolks in March, 1943—four hundred from the 5th battalion and 150 from the 6th. The journey north usually took four or five days. The prisoners travelled in closed steel freight wagons, which in the intense heat became as hot as ovens; they were packed twenty-five to thirty in each wagon, so tightly that it was impossible to lie down or move around. The metal sides became so hot that they burnt any flesh that touched them and the floors of the trucks were often awash with water or covered with coal dust. The Japanese issued only rice for the journey, but sometimes friendly Malaysians gave them fruit. The prisoners suffered dreadfully, and arrived at their destination weak and exhausted.

Base camp for the prisoners working on the railway was at Chungkai, about a hundred miles west of Bangkok, which until their arrival had been an isolated Thai kampong (village) surrounded by dense vegetation at the edge of virgin jungle. In all about 6,000 British prisoners-of-war were sent there.

At Chungkai, and at the other camps to which they moved forward as the work

*This later became known as the "Railway of Death".

proceeded during 1943, they were accommodated in "Attap" huts—flimsy constructions of bamboo, covered with a thatch of dried palm fronds—or under canvas, although sometimes they found themselves forced to bivouac in the open. The Attap huts were about 250 feet long by 26 feet wide, and each had a centre gangway—often a ditch of mud and water—and raised platforms on each side on which the men slept. These platforms were always alive with bugs. Each prisoner was allotted a section of platform about eight feet by four feet. The tents were old and worn, and there was little protection from tropical storms. A monotonous and inadequate diet, mostly of rice, with very few vegetables, and brutal treatment by the camp guards, most of whom were Koreans, compounded their misery.

At Chungkai the Japanese commander held weekly conferences with the British battalion commanders, and soon after each battalion arrived it was given a clear indication of Japanese attitudes. Officers were told that they would have to take a full part in the construction work; they insisted that this was contrary to the Geneva Convention and refused. After delivering an ultimatum, which the officers

The bridge over the River Kwai at Kanchanaburi in Thailand, built by British prisoners of war supervised by Japanese engineers.   *Vic Brown Collection*

Maps showing the course of the Burma–Thailand railway, known later as the Railway of Death.

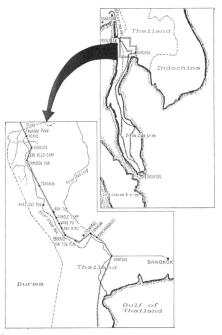

ignored, the Japanese commandant called out the armed Korean guards, who surrounded them. The Cambridgeshire men were the first to undergo this test. Herded into a small clearing, they faced machine-guns and were told that they would be killed if they maintained their refusal. When the Suffolks arrived later, the Korean guards were ostentatiously issued with ammunition for their rifles and ordered to load. In the end, the officers gave way, though the official history of the Suffolk Regiment states: "There had been much feeling in the camp on the subject, some arguing that they should continue to refuse at any cost"[1].

A few of the most senior officers gained their point, after many days of threats, and continued with their command duties, providing leadership to their men. They were permitted to re-form the forces available and to decide their composition. Thus, Lieutenant-Colonel E. L. V. Mapey formed the remnants of the 2nd Cambridgeshires, brought up to the required strength of two hundred men with RAOC personnel, into what henceforth was known as No 5 Work Battalion; Lieutenant-Colonel A. A. Johnson, of the 4th Suffolks, selected seven officers and 250 other ranks from among men of the 4th Suffolks and 4th Royal Norfolks and formed them into No 8 Work Battalion; and Lieutenant-Colonel L. J. Baker, of the 5th Suffolks, formed No 4 Work Battalion. A good number of these work battalions were formed; men of the 5th Royal Norfolks found themselves in No 16 Work Battalion.

From Chungkai the work battalions were sent forward, leap-frogging one another as they worked their way northward into ever more inhospitable country. The work, which was supervised by Japanese engineers, was heavy and exhausting by any standards; for Europeans unaccustomed to the climatic conditions and weakened by inadequate food and sickness it was appalling. The new railway was being built through jungle and over rocky hills and swift-flowing rivers. There was no machinery. The track-bed had to be levelled by hand, using crowbars and sledgehammers. Embankments were constructed of soil and stone which had to be quarried and filled into baskets, then passed along a human chain to the embankment.

A "task system" operated: provided an allotted task was completed in six days, the seventh day was a rest day. But the men were under-nourished on a daily ration

A prison camp on the Kwai seen from the air. The long attap huts in which the prisoners lived can be seen at right angles to the river. *Vic Brown Collection*

of about twenty ounces of rice, twenty ounces of vegetables and less than four ounces of meat, plus two-thirds of an ounce of sugar, one-third of an ounce of salt and one-tenth of an ounce of tea.

They slept fitfully, for the nights were bitterly cold and no-one had more than one blanket or a sack. They were inadequately clothed, often with only a single pair of shorts or a loin cloth, and boots, shoes and hats were very scarce. Conditions in the camps were insanitary. Consequently sickness was endemic, with cholera, beri-beri, malaria, amoebic dysentery and diphtheria; often nearly half the men were often sick at the same time. The regimental doctors did their best, but drugs and medical supplies were in short supply. There were many East Anglian casualties among the 13,000 Europeans who did not survive. Those who did could not hope to meet the demands made by the Japanese, and they were struck, slapped, kicked, and subjected to many indignities.

The prisoners-of-war were forbidden all writing materials, but they frequently contrived to defeat such restrictions. One party of men of the Cambridgeshire Regiment managed, before they were sent north from Singapore, to collect a store of radio components and at the Chungkai camp they encountered an officer of the Royal Corps of Signals who was able to construct five small radio receivers. These were smuggled to the camps strung out along the line of the railway, carefully concealed in water bottles and elsewhere, and morale was greatly boosted by the ability to receive some news from the outside world. Some camps also obtained copies of an English-language newspaper, the *Bangkok Chronicle*; although it was controlled by the Japanese, it was possible to "read between the lines".

Most remarkable of all, however, was the achievement of two officers who managed to keep diaries of events as they moved from camp to camp, Captain R. G. de Quincey, of the Suffolk Regiment, and Dr Robert Hardie, a medical officer with the Federated Malay States Volunteer Force[2].

Captain de Quincey chronicled the tribulations of the No 8 Work Battalion as in January, 1943, it made a three-day march to the camp at Banmau*, then at the end of March went on by train, motor-boat and on foot to what was known as "Jungle Camp", a month later spent nine days marching northward to "Camp 203 Kilo", and then in August moved to "226 Kilo Camp", where this group settled for the remainder of 1943. This diary presents vivid cameos of the prisoners' life, for example, the arrival at Banmau:

> We found the camp situated round a School and Temple, with pleasant trees and grass, and a large village in the vicinity. The camp was only half-built, there being five large huts, of which two were unfinished and only one had bamboo beds in it . . . Captain Anger ran an excellent canteen—eggs were always plentiful—and Sergeant Wiffen ran the shop . . . The Thais, on the whole, were friendly and set up a few native shops in the camp . . .

*In Captain de Quincey's diary it is called Barnkau. The men made up their own phonetic equivalents for place-names as they heard them, so various spellings were used.

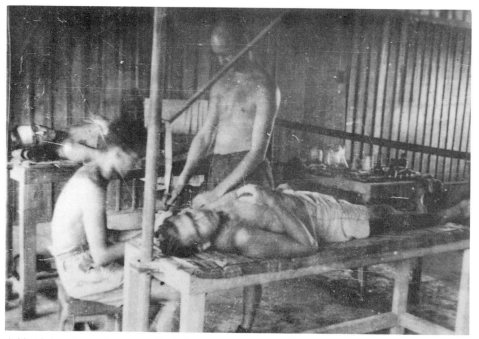

A blood donation under way in the MI room at Temuang. There was a serious shortage of medical supplies, and many of those who became sick had little chance of recovery.　*Vic Brown Collection*

Another account of Banmau presents a much grimmer picture:

The Japanese made no allowance for illness and if the task failed to be completed in the time allowed, the "pickle stick" was brought out. This was a bamboo about two inches in diameter and four feet long. Everyone would receive a taste of it, sometimes for the most trivial of things, such as forgetting to number in Japanese. Many a man was beaten senseless by the stick. On one occasion it was impossible, through illness, to find sufficient labour. The Japs called out all RSMs, lined them up, and really belted into them. Officers were treated hideously. Every morning they were assembled and the "Nip" engineer officer strolled along the ranks, kicking the prisoners and spitting in their faces, doing everything in their power to humiliate them.[3]

After six weeks at Banmau the work battalion was allowed a two-week rest, during which the sick were sent back to base camp at Chungkai. There, Captain de Quincey noted, "from all accounts, conditions and especially the rations are now sufficiently good for the light sick to get well, but are inadequate for the bad sick". The hospital was ill-equipped and overcrowded, and medical supplies were minimal.

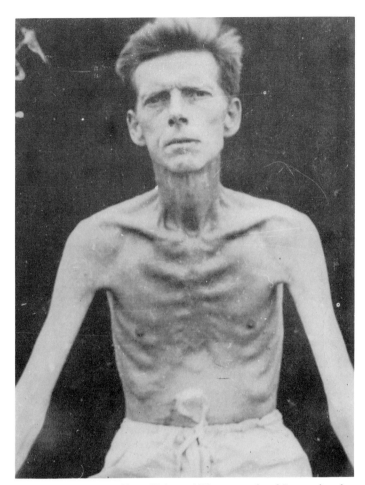

A chronic case of
malnutrition.
Vic Brown Collection

One of the men in No 4 Work Battalion, Edward Hammond, of Ixworth, also kept a diary during this period, from which these poignant extracts are taken:

Thursday, January 14th: It's terribly cold at nights up here and I lie and shiver all night and long for the sun to rise in the morning to get warm. I have no blanket, only a rice sack.

Saturday, January 30th: Just a year ago today since I last heard from my loved ones at home, bless them all.

Monday, February 1st: We must be getting into the Thai summer, as it's terribly hot now. I'm very weak at present. My legs get so tired and ache, I've hardly strength to walk. A lot of the boys are in the most pitiful condition, a lot of Beri Beri . . .

Wednesday, February 3rd: Food very bad indeed . . .

Monday, February 15th: Work again. One year ago today since the fateful day of Singapore's capitulation, and one year of hard work, chiefly on rice. Now we must hope for the best . . .[4]

That was the last entry. Later in the year Edward Hammond died of bacillary dysentery and beri-beri.

By April, 1943, the line had been completed as far as Aru Hiri (Arrowhill) and the Cambridgeshire men in No 5 Work Battalion were sent forward to Wang Po for a short stay blasting and bridge-building. Although this was an area with dense vegetation, there was much activity: barges on the river, towed by small *pom-pom* boats, monkeys playing in the bushes, and a great variety of birds, including kingfishers, bee-eaters, sandpipers, kites and ospreys. In happier circumstances visitors would have found a great deal of interest.

The Suffolk men in No 8 Work Battalion moved further north, to the so-called "Jungle Camp". There Captain de Quincey found things "in a disgraceful condition, excreta everywhere, many bad sick, many ramps, striking prevalent . . .". But he also provides a testimony to the amazing resilience of the prisoners, who set themselves to improve matters. The battalion's Canteen Officer quickly found a Thai

> . . . who behaved generously, bravely and efficiently with our needs, even supplying us with "bird seed" (batteries) for the wireless set. He cashed Colonel Johnson a large cheque, the money from which was later to save many lives of our sick men. Rations improved and the men were well fed, but the work was very long and hard (drilling and blasting) and there were many incidents and strikings . . .

The next move to Takanun ("203 Kilo Camp") involved nine days' marching, seven of them without solid food. The men marched for forty minutes, then rested for twenty. "Much singing en route, especially *The Perambulator* and *Cockadoodle Doo*," Captain de Quincey noted. At "203 Kilo Camp", on a good, sandy site by a river, there was a serious shortage of tents and the guards were very difficult.

Meanwhile, No 4 Work Battalion (5th Suffolks) occupied four or five different camps: Chungkai, where they spent the last few weeks of 1942 quarrying material for the railway embankments; then Wan Tow Kin and Ban Ko (either Banmau or Wang Po) for two months, where the Japanese engineers were truculent and struck blows with bamboo sticks and pick helves and the Korean guards indulged in face-slapping and other indignities; then Kanchanaburi (Canburi), where they ballasted the track that had been laid and found conditions much better; and then Martona, which when they arrived after a four-day march was no more than a strip of wet jungle waiting to be cleared for the erection of tents. Their task there was bridge-building. One of the officers later provided this account of a normal day's work:

> Parade at 8 am. March several miles to work through deep mud, many being barefooted by this time. Pull all day on the ropes of the pile-driver, often in pouring rain, or work high upon the scaffolding, hauling logs into place by hand. Home about 8 pm. Only one break of an hour in the middle of the day. It was not uncommon to see a man fall off the scaffolding from sickness or sheer exhaustion, often aided by a kick or blow from the Japanese engineers. Our diet was boiled rice, three times a day, with dried vegetable, which was invariably rotten. The brutality of the Japanese knew no bounds.[5]

The men of the 4th Work Battalion were by this time in poor shape. Large numbers were sick, but only those with cholera were segregated, the others remaining close-packed in crowded huts, without sanitary provision of any kind. One of the survivors recalled: "It was with difficulty that sufficient numbers could be found to dig the graves and carry the bodies to the graves"—tasks which the CO and other officers undertook. There had been four hundred men in this group when it had left Singapore. By this time there were only 160; seventy had died, and 170 had been sent back sick, many of them to die later.

The Cambridgeshire men in No 5 Work Battalion had also been faring badly. After their bridge-building at Wang Po they marched 120 kilometres in ten days to Takanun, arriving there with very little clothing and their footwear falling apart or, in some cases, lost altogether. Many were suffering from malaria, and all were weak from want of food. There was a small village at Takanun, with houses of wood and thatch and a police station flying the Siamese flag, but the weary prisoners were taken on through orchards growing mangoes, limes, papayas and coconuts to a camp already occupied by a work battalion of Dutchmen, some dying, all in desperate condition. At first there were no Attap huts or tents for the new arrivals and only plain rice and potato tops to eat. Yet the Japanese insisted on

When clothing was reduced to a pair of tattered shorts or merely a loincloth there was little to laugh about, but some prisoners could still raise a smile while preparing a meal for their comrades.

Vic Brown Collection

all but the very sick starting work within twenty-four hours of their arrival in camp, building bridges and embankments and blasting through mountains. Working conditions were horrific. The monsoon rains poured down and everywhere was a sea of mud, in which men often sank up to their knees. Yet they were required to fell large trees, trim them ready for bridge-building and then lash them to the traces of working elephants controlled by Burmese boys. This went on from daybreak to dusk every day, and any slackening of effort was punished by a beating with "pickle sticks".

A lot of men from the eastern counties were at Takanun at much the same time: Cambridgeshire men in No 5 Work Battalion, Norfolk men in No 8 and No 16 Work Battalions, and Suffolk men in No 8 Work Battalion. Dr Hardie arrived there in May and found four hundred of the Norfolks in very squalid tents, with very bad food. He noted that 240 were too sick to work, adding:

> Many are desperately ill with dysentery, beri-beri and pellagra, malaria and exhaustion. The "hospital" is supplied with five Japanese tents with mosquito curtains, which are squat and low, about twelve feet wide and fifteen feet long, and three small leaky Indian-type tents, which are smaller but slightly higher. There are no floorboards.[6]

Cholera broke out in this camp on 23rd May, and by 1st June there were eighty cases and there had been thirty-five deaths. The dead were cremated by their comrades. When some of the Japanese then fell victim to cholera, action was taken: all prisoners who had escaped the illness were moved out a short distance to what was called Takanun "fit camp", where they were put on to a sixteen-hours-a-day working routine. The chronically sick remained behind in the "sick camp", and Dr Hardie noted:

> The Japanese pathologist who has been around in connexion with the cholera has shown himself quite sympathetic, but he has no medical supplies and cannot do much for us.[7]

The testimony of William Taylor is different. He declared that at frequent intervals the Japanese medical officer would pick one at random from among those who could just walk and transfer him to the "fit camp" to work. Ulcers were prevalent, spreading over limbs until they were shocking in appearance, smell and effect on general health, and Taylor states that men with ghastly ulcers who could not stand were sometimes carried to the railway and made to break stones[8]. By June, 1943, with the rain still pouring down daily, conditions had deteriorated beyond description. Even for those who, like Dr Hardie, escaped sickness at this time it was acutely depresssing.

> . . . lying awake at night on a rough bamboo bed a few inches off the damp black soil, which teems with ants, listening to the patter of rain on the leaky tent roof, and the whisper and creak of the bamboo just outside.[9]

For the sick, the nights were full of disturbing sounds: the chirping of cicadas, the croaking of frogs, the rustling of leaves in the wind, the splashing of the rapids in the river below the camp. Here, in this sink of pain and privation, at the darkest hour, something like a miracle occurred. On 23rd June the men received their first letters from home since their capture at Singapore sixteen months earlier.

And, by coincidence, it was in June that relatives of these same men were invited to a series of gatherings to hear a representative of the Far Eastern Section of the British Red Cross, Mr S. G. King, give what little information had come through, hoping it might offer some comfort to the families. The Cambridgeshire Troop Comforts Fund held a huge tea-party in Cambridge Guildhall, where it was disclosed that about a thousand names of prisoners-of-war had been received each week during March and April. In Norwich so many relatives turned up at a similar meeting that the Stuart Hall was filled to capacity and the organisers had hurriedly to take over the adjoining Suckling Hall as well and relay the speeches. In King's Lynn 350 relatives gathered in the Town Hall.

Norfolk, it was revealed, had more prisoners-of-war in the Far East than any other county. Mr King said that mail from the UK was being dealt with in Tokyo by forty British officer prisoners-of-war. The Japanese, he said, were unsympathetic about parcels and no-one could send them. Some attempt was being made to give UK prisoners a higher ration than the Japanese soldier, but it was still only rice, fish, and vegetables.

Prisoners-of-war funds actively raised money throughout the year, and some of the organised events were almost spectacular in scale. Rarely can Suffolk have seen so ambitious or so popular a fête as that in the Abbey Gardens in Bury St Edmunds in July, staffed by five hundred volunteer helpers and attended by over 20,000 people. It raised £2,500 and was a great community "day out", with a list of attractions ranging from a barrel organ played by a local clergyman to the band of the Suffolk Regiment and from an American Army juggler to a demonstration of gundogs at work.

By July postcards were being received in good numbers, all with a standard message that the sender was in good health and was being well—or at least satisfactorily—treated. It was probably as well that the real sufferings of the men in the prison camps were not known, for by this time over ten thousand were so sick that they had been sent back to the camps at the southern end of the railway: Chungkai, Tamakan and Kanchanaburi.

Men of the 4th Royal Norfolks and of the 4th Suffolks were still at Takanun, and it was there that the Suffolk men celebrated Minden Day on 1st August, the anniversary of a battle in 1759 when their predecessors in the regiment, fighting as part of the Anglo-Prussian alliance, routed a French army. Now, in the jungle of Thailand, the anniversary was celebrated with an issue of ten cigarettes to each man and an evening conjuring show by their medical officer, Captain Lewis, RAMC.

Four days later they faced a painful experience when a new work battalion began to trudge into the camp as darkness fell; they discovered that these were men of the 5th Suffolks, now designated No 4 Work Battalion, led by Lieutenant-

67

A stitch in time. . . The interior of one of the huts in the senior officers' camp at Kanchanaburi.
Vic Brown Collection

Colonel L. J. Baker. This unexpected encounter between men from the same regiment should have been a joyful occasion; it proved painful because of the condition of the new arrivals.

It was, by a cruel coincidence, on Minden Day that No 4 Work Battalion had been ordered up country to Konkuta (which they called Conkwita), accompanied by a large party of Dutch prisoners-of-war. It was a two-week march through sodden jungle and swollen rivers, and only two Japanese guards accompanied them; orders were to "go as you please".

The column was generally about two miles long. The mud was ankle-deep and sucked the soles off men's boots. The rain poured down continuously for four or five days at a time, stopped for two days, then restarted. Water dripped incessantly from the jungle leaves. The mournful crying of many monkeys was incessant. At night the men slept in the jungle, in the open and under the rain. On one day they were left to their own devices to cross three rivers, which non-swimmers managed by balancing perilously on a submerged tree which the swimmers pushed across.

There was only rice and dried vegetables to eat, and the men were lucky if they could start each day with one pint of boiled water in their bottles, though if they could manage to hold their mess tins before them as they marched they could half fill them with rainwater in a few minutes.

They arrived at Takanun on a pitch-black night to find that the track to the camp was a shambles of half-finished bridges and cuttings. Major C. J. M. Watts, who was one of the party, afterwards recalled:

> Here everything was laid on for us. Major Flick and the other 4th Suffolk officers saw to the feeding and housing of the men, and had guides on the track all night guiding stragglers to the camp. Everyone was dead beat and we shall never forget the wonderful reception and kind treatment by the 4th Suffolk. The last of our party, who had sick men with them who could hardly walk, arrived at 0730 on the following morning.[10]

At 2 pm orders were given to proceed. Three men were quite incapable of moving on; as they lay on the ground helpless and Lieutenant-Colonel Johnson, the "resident" Suffolk commander, pleaded for them, two of them were brutally kicked by the guards. In the end they were permitted to remain; within a few days all three had died of cholera.

No 4 Work Battalion moved on. They arrived at the next staging camp on a day when there had been thirteen deaths from cholera, so they were not allowed to enter and spent the night in the open, very cold and wet. Next day they marched on, in streaming rain. Major Watts recalled:

> Most by now had discarded a great part of their kit, as it was too heavy to carry. Nearly everyone was suffering from red and blistered feet. No-one had dry socks or boots during the whole eight days' march. That night we camped at Tamuron Par. The last two miles was a stretch of churned-up mud that came half-way up our legs. Many men fell out, dead-beat, and had to be left behind.
>
> The next stage was to Criam Cri, with an enormous mountain to cross—up and up, sometimes on hands and knees. Finally, as dark fell, many men were benighted on the mountainside, unable to find a way down in the dark.
>
> The last and final day was comparatively easy going, and the party, everyone many pounds lighter in weight, and all suffering from either dysentery, malaria or beri-beri, staggered into Konkuta . . .[11]

There they remained for the rest of the year, at the end of which more than a quarter of them had died.

In London in mid-August the Ministry of Information called a press conference to assert that everything possible was being done to lessen the acute anxiety of the relatives, who still knew nothing of the circumstances of their menfolk. The Ministry implied that the Japanese were not doing their best. As well as using the official channels, the British authorities were monitoring Japanese broadcasts, which sometimes contained names of prisoners-of-war. One of the main problems, a Red Cross representative later explained, was that the Japanese were short of censors able to read English. That was why all letters had to be typed or written in block capitals. In September it was announced that the Japanese authorities also insisted that all letters and post-cards to prisoners should be limited to twenty-five words "to simplify the work of their censorship, so that the correspondence can be speeded up".

Meanwhile the men of the 4th Suffolks in No 8 Work Battalion fared a little better. They left Takanun—the scene of their reunion with the 5th Suffolk men—on 22nd August and Captain de Quincey's diary noted that before leaving all ranks were given some form of footwear. But many lost their plimsolls or shoes in the mud. The march included such obstacles as bridges, ravines, waterfalls, virgin jungle—and mud. There were "thousands of natives all over the place".

They arrived at "226 Kilo Camp" the next day, and there they remained for the rest of the year. Captain de Quincey thought it one of the best-run and happiest camps in Thailand:

> The work and conditions were very hard to start with, but everything possible was done, until eventually the accommodation was good and especially clean, the men's spirits very high, entertainment plentiful, and the messing well run. The chief disadvantages: the dread of cholera and later malignant malaria.

The CO, Lieutenant-Colonel Johnson, was called upon to conduct many burial services. The work on the railway remained hard and the hours long, but by mid-October word spread that construction had been completed, and at about the same time a second batch of mail arrived from England. A Japanese military band travelled up the line giving performances here and there, and on 24th October Dr Hardie noted that:

> . . . A small train went through, with some truckloads of high Nipponese officers, sitting on chairs in open goods wagons specially rigged up with carpentered frames carrying attap roofs. They are said to be going up for the ceremony which is to be held at the linking of the rails. [12]

A week or so later the railway was officially opened; the Japanese gave the prisoners one day's holiday and a special issue of tinned milk, margarine and fish, and the men of Suffolk celebrated in their own way with a "jungle concert". They were still in the camp at Christmas, and Captain de Quincey wrote in his diary:

> Considering the circumstances, the food, sports and entertainment were excellent. Christmas Day included Carols, Treasure Hunt, Magic, Sports, and a most amusing Pantomime.

The Cambridgeshire men of No 5 Work Battalion remained throughout the year in the camp at Takanun, and there were only two days in all the long months when their spirits were briefly lifted: one when their padre, Captain Noel Duckworth, appeared unexpectedly, passing through with a large party of other prisoners on their way to an equally appalling camp at Nikhi, the other when the news came through to the prisoners that Allied forces had invaded Sicily.

The experiences of men of other regiments were less well recorded, but could not have differed greatly. Nikhi, one of the most northerly camps, close to the

Burmese border, was reputed to be one of the worst; very few of the 180 men who were sent there survived the experience.

Back in England in October a representative of the Far Eastern Section of the British Red Cross addressed meetings of relatives and friends in Ipswich and Bury St Edmunds, trying to explain why families had heard nothing from their menfolk. Letters from Malaya, he said, were sent 3,000 miles to Japan, then across Siberia to Moscow, then via two neutral countries, Switzerland and Portugal, to Britain. This could take six to nine months. The Japanese were short of shipping and their mail services were disorganised. Privates were allowed to write only one letter every four months.

The Red Cross also reported that the Japanese paid their prisoners-of-war three-halfpence to sixpence a day for the work they were required to perform, and this money could be spent in non-profitmaking canteens, where such sums purchased more than they would in the United Kingdom. The Red Cross had sent 3,500 tons of food, medicines and clothing, and hoped to send more.

The Japanese published a newspaper in English, and the speaker at the Ipswich and Bury meetings expressed confidence that the prisoners were able to "read between the lines", so that they would know that Mussolini had fallen, that Italy had been invaded, and that Britain was not losing the war. As they had been

The lack of adequate clothing is evident from this photograph of "peanut bashing" in the senior officers' camp at **Kanchanaburi**. *Vic Brown Collection*

captured at the moment when Britain's fortunes were at their lowest this was an important point. For the thousands of wives and mothers who attended, or read reports of, these meetings, the most comforting thing was a declaration that "to the present, there is no evidence of a single case of atrocity".

Once the railway had been completed, most of the prisoners-of-war were transferred; men of the East Anglian regiments found themslves split up and sent all over the Pacific. Some of the prison ships in which they sailed were torpedoed; in one such incident one officer and ninety men of the 2nd battalion of the Cambridgeshire Regiment lost their lives. There were also casualties among the men who were not quickly transferred from Thailand, because Allied planes began to bomb the newly-completed railway.

By the end of 1943 the Red Cross still had only 30,000 names. That left 22,000 "missing", and although they were sure there could not have been 22,000 casualties it left 22,000 families in suspense after nearly two years without reliable news.

There were some East Anglians who did not reach Singapore and were spared captivity. After the initial Japanese victories in the Far East, a threat to India was perceived. The 1st Battalion, Essex Regiment, which had fought at Tobruk, was part of the 70th Division, which arrived in India in March, 1943. It was the only trained, battle-experienced formation in India at the time, and it was held in reserve to provide a mobile striking force against any Japanese landing on the coast of Bengal between Calcutta and Cuttack. In May it moved forward into Arakan

and made its base at Bawli Bazaar, where it learned to cope with mule transport and spent several weeks holding a pass in rough mountain country.

In September the 23rd Infantry Brigade, of which the 1st Essex was part, became a special force under the command of Major-General Orde Wingate, who had pioneered methods of long-range penetration in enemy-held jungle country. The first of these "Chindit" operations had been judged sufficiently successful to merit expansion to a strength equivalent to two divisions, with its own No 1 Air Commando unit at eleven-squadron strength, and the Essex men now joined this elite force. All men over forty were posted away. The 1st Essex was formed into two columns, each with eighteen officers and about four hundred other ranks, each column completely self-contained, using mule transport and depending upon supplies by air. Intensive training took place in the Central Provinces, supervised by Wingate, during which the monsoon broke. The columns operated in jungle conditions, 5,000 feet up, in swirling cloud most of the day; sometimes the supply planes, guided in by radio at five-day intervals, failed to deliver because of the conditions, and men were left exhausted, hungry and sick. This punishing training was still going on at the end of the year.

Meanwhile the Japanese strengthened their hold on Burma. In August South East Asia Command was formed, with Admiral Lord Louis Mountbatten as Supreme Commander. The 2nd Battalion of the Royal Norfolks formed a part of the forces which prepared to ward off any enemy assault. This battalion had been

Opposite page: Carried on a timber viaduct, the Burma–Thailand railway skirts a rocky bluff at Tam Krasaer in Thailand.
Vic Brown Collection

Right: A cutting through rock at Kanchanaburi.
Vic Brown Collection

decimated at Dunkirk in 1940, after which it was re-formed and kept busy on anti-invasion exercises while it awaited new equipment and its next overseas posting. It had arrived in India in June, 1942, as part of the 2nd Infantry Division. It was now stationed in the area of Ahmadnagar, some 125 miles inland from Bombay, and at regular intervals it went down to the coast to take part in large-scale assault training on the beaches.

For the 2nd Royal Norfolks the year ended on a note of frustration. Mountbatten planned to strike at the extended Japanese lines of communication, and for this purpose he wanted air and naval bases on the Andaman Islands, in the Bay of Bengal between Burma and India. "Operation Buccaneer" was designed as a major assault on the islands; but it had to be cancelled when many assault craft were reassigned to the coming invasion of Europe. A more modest operation, "Pigstick", was then put in hand—a landing behind the forward Japanese lines near Akyab, in Burma—and this kept senior officers busy until the year-end. The Officer Commanding the Norfolks was among those who were in conference in Bombay in December*.

The 2nd Battalion, the Suffolk Regiment also spent the whole of 1943 in India. Throughout the previous year it had been engaged on internal security operations at Rawalpindi, Lahore and Lucknow, and the official regimental history records that "villages had been burnt, fines collected, roads and railways patrolled. Fire had had to be opened more than once".

From April, 1943, however, the battalion was directed to turn its attention to the coming battle against the Japanese, who stood on the north-eastern border. It was concentrated at Fyzabad, and reorganisation, training and re-equipment began. It suffered from attrition when, first, 150 trained older soldiers were transferred to another regiment, and then twenty-two full-rank NCOs were repatriated. Those who remained moved to the Ranchi area for final intensive training in jungle warfare and spent the monsoon season crawling through paddy fields doing their best to escape drowning. Tents were a luxury; most of them had to make do with a thick bush and a groundsheet.

Elsewhere, Allied forces were recapturing territory which had been occupied by the Japanese. By September, 1943, the Americans had established aerial supremacy in the Pacific zone and the Japanese, sensing a deteriorating and increasingly precarious military situation, were withdrawing to a more compact defensive arc. In November the Americans landed successfully on Bougainville, one of the Solomon Islands, and in December on New Britain, the island on which Rabaul was situated. The net was closing.

*This operation, too, had to be called off soon after, when ALL assault craft were recalled to Europe.

CHAPTER FIVE

The Fighting Fronts

MEN OF the East Anglian regiments were heavily engaged in the fighting in North Africa and in Italy during 1943, and their families back home saw clear evidence of their victories as a trickle of Italian prisoners-of-war into the eastern counties, which had begun the previous year, swelled to a flood during the summer months. At the beginning of the year 8,000 were already housed in eleven camps in the Eastern Command area, and all these camps were extended and several new ones built to receive 44,000 more Italians arriving during 1943. The principal camps were at Barton Field, Ely; Botesdale, near Diss; High Garrett, Braintree; Royston; Sawtry, Hunts; and Trumpington, Cambridge, each with accommodation for 750 prisoners. New camps were built during the year at Fakenham and Lakenheath. Apart from the main camps, there were hostels in many towns and villages, including Balsham, Belchamp Walter, Bourn, Boxford, Elsworth, Feltwell Fen, Finchingfield, Harleston, Kentford, Long Stratton, Newmarket, Pebmarsh, Sible Hedingham and Thetford[1].

The important Allied victory at El Alamein rounded off 1942 and ended the German threat to Egypt. Documentary film of the Eighth Army's desert victory, shot by the Army Film Photographic Unit and the RAF Film Production Unit, was made into a full-length feature film under that title, and was a great box office draw all over Britain. It ran for six days during March and April at most of the cinemas in the eastern counties.

British and American armies had invaded Morocco and Algeria at the western end of the Mediterranean in November, 1942, had captured Casablanca and Algiers, and within a few weeks were within fifteen miles of Tunisia's western frontier. They were then halted by a combination of bad weather, inadequate striking power, and strong reinforcements poured in by the Germans, who had virtually taken over the North African battle from their battered Italian allies. Meanwhile Montgomery's Eighth Army, advancing from the east, forced Rommel to withdraw during January, first to the eastern frontier of Tunisia, and then a further eighty miles to the fortified Mareth Line. Montgomery's leading division did not cross the frontier, however, until 16th February.

By that time the strains developing on Italy's home front were shown by the dismissal on 5th February of the Foreign Minister, Count Ciano. Mussolini, his father-in-law, took over the job himself.

Great convoys now carried men and supplies from the UK, but the build-up was slow because of the limited amount of available shipping. One convoy, which sailed from the Clyde on 24th January, carried what had formerly been the 7th

Battalion of the Cambridgeshires but had now been metamorphosed into the 142nd Regiment of the Royal Armoured Corps. From their traditional infantry role the Cambridgeshire men had changed in November, 1941, to become part of the 25th Army Tank Brigade, equipped with Churchill tanks. After continuous training throughout 1942, they found themselves at the end of the year at Heveningham Hall, near Halesworth, ready for action in close support of infantry. They landed at Algiers on 1st February, and had not long to wait to put their training to the test. After the winter stalemate the Germans attacked in mid-February, aiming to force an Allied retreat into Algeria. They gained ground near Medjez el Bab, captured or disabled two hundred tanks, and within a week were behind the Allies' forward defence line. There was some confusion, much rushing up of reinforcements, and fierce fighting.

The 142nd Regiment had barely completed the unloading of its tanks when it was ordered into action on 21st February. It played some part in beating off the enemy attack, and during the following few weeks it found itself frequently dispersed, sometimes in squadron strength, sometimes in smaller units, to assist other detached formations in regrouping and reoccupying lost ground.

By this time another East Anglian regiment was deeply involved at the eastern end of the battle. The 1st/4th Battalion, Essex Regiment had already greatly distinguished itself during the North African fighting when, as part of the 4th Indian Division, it had engaged in heavy desert battles against Rommel's forces and played an important role at El Alamein in November, 1942. As the new year opened it was moving forward to Benghazi. Here it underwent training for the very different terrain that lay ahead—mountain, hill and river—and also for street fighting.

The Essex battalion made contact with Rommel's rearguard south-east of the Mareth Line on 8th March. Twelve days later Montgomery launched a frontal attack on this defence barrier which failed, and so he decided to extend the front by occupying the high ground westward. In this outflanking move the 4th Indian Division moved sideways and inland to clear a pass through the Matmata Hills and then pushed northwards along the hilltops, a difficult task but one which their training in hill and night fighting enabled them to complete with conspicuous success. The advance began at nightfall on 5th April, and before dawn they had made a deep penetration into the hills and taken 4,000 prisoners. They then made a frontal attack on a strong position to which the Germans had retreated, after which the commander of the force declared confidently: "We have broken the enemy and the way is clear for 10 Corps to go through." He suggested that immediate offensive action would finish the North African campaign[2]. The follow-up was delayed, however, and the chance of a decisive victory lost; the Axis troops were able to withdraw 150 miles northwards to defend a hundred-mile arc from the north coast to the coast south of Enfidaville.

Patrols of Montgomery's Eighth Army advancing from the east and Americans

The advance on Tunis, March to May, and the movements of the 1st/4th Battalion, The Essex Regiment.

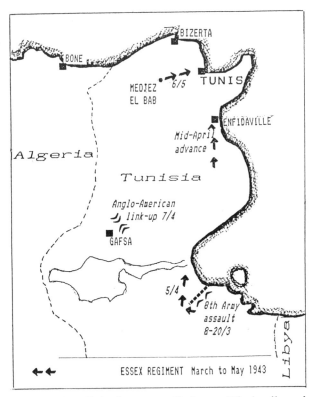

who had landed in North West Africa first linked up near Gafsa on 7th April, and this sealed the fate of Tunis. The Eighth Army occupied a chain of coastal towns in quick succession, and within a week was in the area of Enfidaville. The Essex Regiment was called forward to occupy the area south-west of Enfidaville, where it was engaged in four days and nights of bitter, heavy fighting, losing four killed and seventy-six wounded before being moved into reserve, "battered but indomitable".

The Allies now prepared a plan for a knockout blow, a general offensive on every sector with the main effort near Medjez el Bab. The 4th Indian Division and the 7th Armoured Division were switched from the Enfidaville sector to the Medjez el Bab sector for this operation, which was launched on 6th May. The Essex battalion, with an escort of thirty tanks, sailed through first, opening the way, so that by 9.30 am that day the 4th Indian Division was able to punch a deep hole in the enemy lines and report back to the Corps HQ that the armour could "go as fast and as far as it liked"[3]. Again there was a failure to exploit the situation, but just before 4 pm on 7th May armoured cars of the 11th Hussars drove into Tunis, and the city was occupied that day. In fact, the Axis army had run out of fuel, ammunition and food and its supply lines had been cut.

The Cambridgeshire men of the 142nd Regiment, Royal Armoured Corps,

This photograph of light A.A. gunners from Norwich and Norfolk serving in the Middle East comes from Sgt. H. E. Cooper, R.A., who is in the centre row. He adds: "Please tell our families and friends we are all well and in the best of spirits, looking forward to the day when we shall be home again."

Names of the gunners are as follow: Left to right (back row)—Gnrs. Simnet (Yarmouth), Gunn (Yarmouth), Davy (Lamas), Denny (Beccles), L/Bdr. Bane (Suffield Park). Centre—Bdr. Moore (Norwich), Sgt. Hewitt (Yarmouth), Sgt. Cooper (North Walsham), Bdr. Payne (Norwich). Front—Gnrs. Bilham (Norwich), Howes (Costessey), Bell (Norwich).

Newspapers often contained photographs of local men serving overseas. This group of light AA gunners all came from the northern part of East Anglia and were serving in the Middle East.

Eastern Evening News

which had again been concentrated as a unit, were also engaged in the intense fighting to open the road to Tunis during most of April, in the sector north-east of Medjez el Bab.

On 8th May the *East Anglian Daily Times* front page proclaimed:

BIZERTA AND TUNIS ARE IN ALLIED HANDS

**First Army reaches its goals within 48 hours
of launching offensive**

and two days later:

FIFTY THOUSAND PRISONERS IN TUNISIA

General Alexander, who had taken command of all Allied land forces engaged in the campaign, signalled Prime Minister Churchill on 13th May: "All enemy resistance has ceased. We are masters of the North African shores." And Churchill, addressing the United States Congress a few days later, declared: "Arrived at this milestone in the war, we can say, 'One continent redeemed.'"

Both the Essex and the Cambridgeshire regiments played a part in the mopping up of the last scattered remnants of Hitler's African army and the collection of prisoners, and then they were able to move up beside the Mediterranean for a period of relaxation. The Essex battalion spent the rest of May and the first part of June at Misurata, and the Cambridgeshire men of the 142nd Regiment concentrated in some pleasant olive groves, with magnificent bathing facilities, within easy reach of Tunis. The Cambridgeshire men took part in the Victory Parade in Tunis on 20th May; some were in the march-past, some formed a flanking guard for the saluting base, some lined part of the route. Nearly a month later, on 19th June, the Essex men paraded on the Tripoli–Castel Benito road for inspection by King George VI, who had flown out from England.

By that time the victory had been celebrated in Britain. The *East Anglian Daily Times* reported on 14th May:

> The government have been in consultation with the leaders of the churches and all clergy and ministers are asked at their services on Sunday next, May 16th, to offer special prayers of thanksgiving for the victory granted to the forces of the Commonwealth and Empire and of our Allies in Africa. It is hoped that wherever practicable church bells throughout the county will be pealed.

The Cambridgeshire men of the 25th Tank Brigade moved to Ain Mokra, near Bone, in Algeria. One hundred men were granted leave in the United Kingdom, some others at rest camps near the sea, and others again were used to escort prisoners-of-war to Britain, after which they were granted several weeks' home leave, returning to North Africa in September and October. The regiment returned to Tunisia in September for further training, with the 24th Guards Brigade and with units of the 1st Free French Division, but by the end of November it was back with the remainder of the 25th Tank Brigade near Bone.

The African war over, attention turned immediately to Italy. Throughout the first half of 1943 newspaper headlines built up a fever of expectation until on 9th June the *East Anglian Daily Times* front page lead gave some official credence:

PREMIER TELLS COMMONS OF BIG COMING OPERATIONS

This was followed by the news of the visit by the King, with his Secretary for War and Air Minister, to British forces in North Africa, and simultaneously reports that Allied air forces were making day-long assaults on Sicilian aerodromes. By the end of June the King was back in Britain and the headlines gave the Italians notice:

ALLIES' MEDITERRANEAN PREPARATIONS NEAR COMPLETION

The invasion of Sicily was not long coming. The *East Anglian Daily Times* front page on 12th July carried these headlines:

ALLIES TAKE THREE SICILIAN AIRFIELDS
Forces steadily pushing inland from the beaches
LINKED ALONG 100 MILES INVASION COAST

A week later it was learned that Hitler and Mussolini had been in conference in Northern Italy, which was interpreted as a sure sign that the Axis knew it was in difficulties. Now followed a steady succession of stories of Allied successes. On 16th July Algiers Radio repeatedly broadcast a joint message from Churchill and Roosevelt addressed to the Italian people: "The time has come for you to decide whether Italians shall die for Mussolini and Hitler—or live for Italy and for civilisation." At this stage about a third of Sicily had been taken. On 19th July—the same day as the dictators' get-together—Rome had had its first air raid. Within a week came the dramatic denouement:

MUSSOLINI RESIGNS HIS PREMIERSHIP

read the front page headlines in the *East Anglian Daily Times* on the 26th. By mid-August the air assault had been developed, so that the 14th August *East Anglian Daily Times* headlines read:

ALLIED AIR ARMADAS BLAST ROME, MILAN AND TURIN
Our bombers switch to Italy: Three great assaults in 12 hours

On Friday, 3rd September, before dawn—the fourth anniversary of the outbreak of the war—Allied armies invaded the southern shores of Italy and so returned to the mainland of Europe. The *East Anglian Daily Times* headlined:

EIGHTH ARMY BATTLING INLAND FROM REGGIO BEACHES
Germans talk of fierce fighting after British landing on Italian mainland

This was followed only five days later by these headlines:

ITALY LAYS DOWN HER ARMS
"Unconditional surrender" announced by General Eisenhower

Hopes ran high that the Allied armies would be in Rome before the year ended, but more German troops were moved into Italy and under Field Marshal Kesselring's command put up fierce resistance, so that on the last day of December the Allies were still a hundred miles from the Italian capital.

The main landing by Montgomery's troops was at the "toe" of Italy, with a secondary landing at Taranto, an important port at the "heel", from where troops were required to advance northwards up the east coast to occupy the ports of Brindisi and Bari. Nearly three weeks was spent settling in at Taranto, and Eighth Army reinforcements then began to arrive, from 22nd September. The 19th Infantry Brigade of the 8th Indian Division, of which the 1st/5th battalion of the Essex Regiment was a part, were among the first.

The 1st/5th Essex had until May, 1943, been in Iraq and Persia, and had then moved to Syria and undergone training in hill warfare. It had been greatly diluted during this period, so that it included men from more than thirty different regiments. Now it was destined to do some of the fiercest fighting in the early stages of the Italian campaign.

At first the Eighth Army encountered virtually no opposition as it moved northward, first to Bari and then to Foggia, 120 miles from Taranto. Early in October the Essex battalion was ordered to move on ahead of the 8th Indian Division to stop looting and restore order in heavily-bombed Foggia, which was in some chaos, without electric light, water and medical services. Lieutenant-Colonel B. G. Allen, second-in-command of the battalion, was installed as Military Governor of the town, with the assistance of a single interpreter, Private Tatti, who assumed the responsibilities of policing and security and ran three improvised prisons. They found an American engineer who managed partially to restore water and electricity.

Lieutenant-Colonel Allen remained in Foggia as town major while the rest of the battalion continued to advance, reaching the river Trigno without meeting serious opposition. "There was no physical contact and it was difficult to convince the man in the ranks that there was, in fact, nothing between him and the enemy."[4]

Things were soon to take on a much more exciting aspect. An attempt was to be made to cross the wide Trigno at dawn on 2nd November to establish a bridgehead and then, with the support of tanks, to pursue the enemy. The official historian of the regiment recorded that:

> Few slept that night. It was the first battle, and there was natural anxiety, coupled with physical discomfort. The fleas and the weather were against sleep . . . To make matters worse, there was that night an extremely thick mist, which reduced visibility to from five to twenty yards.[5]

As soon as the leading elements went into the river they came under heavy and accurate fire from artillery, machine-guns and mortars. They were up against the best-trained and toughest German troops in Italy, entrenched in a carefully prepared position. Those who got across the river found their radio link had failed, and in the dark, the smoke and the mist all the plans began to go awry. By nightfall the Essex battalion had been driven back across the river, having suffered 139 casualties, including ten officers and forty-one NCOs. Despite this setback, a patrol crossed the river again three days later and found the Germans withdrawing. So the battalion crossed and advanced five miles to the little hilltop town of Palmoli, where they halted for five days.

The Germans withdrew seventeen miles to the next river barrier, the Sangro, and the Essex battalion was kept in a forward position as the Eighth Army pursued them. Montgomery hoped to strike a vital blow at the Germans here by smashing their winter line and advancing far enough to threaten the rear of the enemy forces, which were delaying the Fifth Army's advance northward from its landing beaches at Salerno up the west coast towards Rome.

The weather was bad and the attempt at the river crossing was delayed for several days, but during the night of 23rd November the 1st/5th Essex was ordered forward. A mighty current was flowing and it was raining hard, but the men struggled across and advanced to capture their first objective, a village which dominated the crossing, but not before their strength had been depleted by a hundred men killed, wounded or missing. They then found themselves in an unforeseen predicament: the river had risen and the battalion was cut off from the forces which were to have followed it over, including tanks and anti-tank guns. They spent four uneasy days before a crossing was possible.

There was much worse ahead. The Germans retired to a main line further back and brought up panzer reinforcement; the fighting became harder and the advance was halted. On 22nd December the Essex men were ordered to attack the village of Villa Grande, which (although they did not know it) was held by the German 1st Parachute Division. They fought their way through heavy defensive fire, reached the village, and found that every building in it was a fortress, so that they had to fight their way from house to house, cellar to loft, every yard contested. The battle continued for seven days, "a costly and harrowing experience"[6]. German defenders put out Red Cross flags and there was a brief respite while each side collected its wounded. Then battle began again. During the night of 27th/28th the Germans withdrew from the village, which was captured on the 28th, by which time it was strewn with corpses. The Essex battalion's casualties totalled thirteen officers and 266 other ranks.

It was heroic, but was it necessary? The historian of the Essex Regiment summed up:

> A high price had been paid for relatively unimportant gains, and the need to sacrifice so much for so little of strategic importance can be fairly questioned.[7]

His doubts were shared by the Chief of Staff of the Eighth Army, Major-General Sir Francis De Guingand, who with hindsight reached the conclusion:

> Had we gone on too long? Were troops being driven too hard? I feel very definitely that a mistake was made in pressing the Sangro offensive as far as it was. When once the weather had broken, it was extremely unlikely that we could have advanced across the mountains . . .[8]

Other East Anglian regiments which were involved in the Italian campaign during this period fared better. With Allied armies advancing on the Italian mainland, the North African bases and the harbours in Sicily assumed great importance as they handled movements of men, armour and supplies in steadily increasing numbers. Two battalions arrived in September, 1943, to play a part in maintaining the lines of communication: the 30th Battalion of the Royal Norfolks and the 31st Battalion of the Cambridgeshires, who sailed on the same vessel from the Clyde to Algiers. Both had recently been reorganised and designated second-line service battalions.

Operations by East Anglian regiments in Italy between September and December.

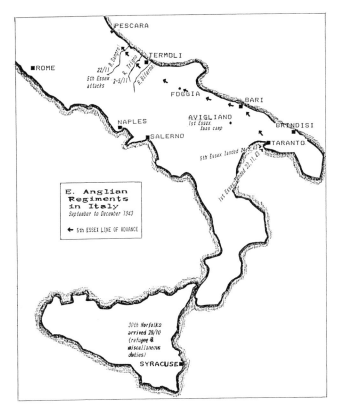

The Norfolks spent the first ten days guarding Italian prisoners-of-war who had been formed into working parties in the docks. They then moved 200 miles eastwards along the coast to Bone to a large supply depot. The Arab labourers who were employed there had organised a flourishing black market in some of the stores, and the Norfolks were assigned to the task of restoring order. The regimental historian wrote:

> The battalion, before taking over their new duties, underwent a fair amount of training, to learn most of the tricks at which the Arabs were past masters, and thus to counter them.[9]

But having learnt the tricks, and before they could begin their new duties, the battalion was on the move again, for garrison duties in Sicily. It reached Syracuse, the main port for the Allies, on 28th October, and soon afterwards it blossomed a new identity, becoming known as the 152nd Brigade, part of the 40th Division. This was in fact a phantom division, created simply as part of a bluff which it was hoped would confuse the enemy. Each of the battalion headquarters was disguised as a brigade HQ; COs became brigadiers and adjutants brigade majors—but only on paper, for they did not wear these badges of rank. During the remainder of the year the battalion did a variety of odd jobs, such as staffing a refugee camp at Syracuse.

The 31st battalion of the Cambridgeshires, after disembarkation at Algiers, proceeded by train to Bizerta. Officers and warrant officers travelled in coaches, but for the men, jolted about in cattle trucks, it was a tough journey spread over four nights. They cooked their meals on station platforms when the train halted. At Bizerta they took over responsibility for a busy concentration area for troops in transit from Africa to Italy, and they also had prisoners-of-war duties.

The 1st Battalion of the Essex Regiment, meanwhile, having endured the heavy fighting in Tunisia, had moved by easy stages during late June and early July back to Alexandria. From there it sailed to Taranto, arriving on 22nd November and spending Christmas under training, in appalling conditions, at Avigliano.

News of the final victory in Africa and of the successful invasion of Italy was avidly followed by relatives and friends of those taking part, in regional newspapers, on the radio, and through newsreel films shown in the cinemas. But there was equal interest throughout 1943 in a battle-front far away, in eastern Europe, though no British forces were directly involved. German invaders had made their maximum occupation of Russian soil during 1942, reaching the gates of Moscow, holding Leningrad under siege, and advancing to the Volga near Stalingrad. The way in which the Red Army had fought back and turned the tide had surprised the Allied governments and earned the unstinted admiration of the people. News from the Eastern Front dominated the headlines as 1943 began; the front page of the *East Anglian Daily Times* on New Year's Day reported:

NAZIS LOSE 312,000 MEN IN THREE GREAT BATTLES
Russians kill 175,000, capture 137,000, on Don and Stalingrad fronts

There seemed to be a special fascination with numbers. The *Cambridge Daily News* front-page headlines on 6th January were:

500,000 GERMANS IN FULL RETREAT
Red Army advancing in all directions on Middle Don front

The Russians were certainly on the offensive. In the north the Red Army relieved the pressure on Leningrad, punching a hole in the seventeen-month-old German ring around the city. The *East Anglian Daily Times* headlines on 19th January read:

LENINGRAD RELIEVED BY VICTORIOUS RED ARMY

Further south, the Germans had been pushed back from Moscow and Stalingrad had been recaptured before the end of 1942. In the new year, only a small pocket of German troops who had been ordered by Hitler not to retreat were holding out near Stalingrad; and on 31st January the German commander there, Field Marshal Paulus, surrendered. The *Cambridge Daily News* reported:

OVER 300,000 LOST AT STALINGRAD
Paulus and 16 Generals captured

At about the same time the whole "Group A" German army in the Caucasus was in danger of being cut off and "caught in a bag", but in the end it escaped the net and successfully withdrew, crossing the River Don at Rostov and moving westwards. In the central sector the Russians drove westward from the Don during February and approached Kursk and Kharkov, the springboard area from which the Germans had begun their eastwards offensive the previous summer.

Mr Ernest Bevin, the Minister of Labour, summed up: "The tide has turned – the Axis Powers are moving to the defensive." Mass Observation, which reported regularly on the state of public morale, described the situation:

> During January cheerfulness remained at its high level of last month . . . With the continued success of the Russians, there was a growing optimism about the likely length of the war . . .

The optimism and the cheerfulness found enthusiastic expression when the 25th anniversary of the creation of the Red Army was celebrated, with much ceremonial, in Cambridge in February. Every town and village in Norfolk, Suffolk,

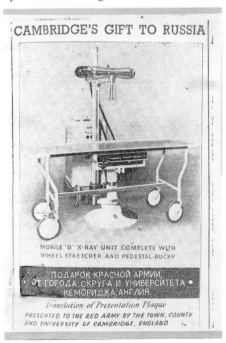

CAMBRIDGE'S GIFT TO RUSSIA

MOBILE 'D' X-RAY UNIT COMPLETE WITH WHEEL STRETCHER AND PEDESTAL-BUCKY

ПОДАРОК КРАСНОЙ АРМИИ, ОТ ГОРОДА, ОКРУГА И УНИВЕРСИТЕТА КЕМБРИДЖА, АНГЛИЯ.

Translation of Presentation Plaque
PRESENTED TO THE RED ARMY BY THE TOWN, COUNTY AND UNIVERSITY OF CAMBRIDGE, ENGLAND

Admiration for the Russian war effort led many East Anglian towns to raise money to send medical and other supplies. Cambridge sent a mobile X-ray unit.   *Cambridge Local Collection*

The only A.T.S. Band in the country passing the Bull Hotel (now an American Red Cross Services Club) before an appreciative audience of American troops.

An ATS band was among those which took part in a parade in Cambridge celebrating the 25th anniversary of the creation of the Red Army. *Cambridge Local Collection*

Essex, Bedfordshire, Hertfordshire, Huntingdonshire and Cambridgeshire was represented in a mile-long procession through the streets, their mayors and chairmen wearing chains of office, representatives of all the Services marching behind six bands, and every section of civilian life taking part, including several hundred munition workers in overalls, dungarees, dustcoats and smocks. There were four thousand in the march, and they took twenty minutes to pass the saluting base at the Fitzwilliam Museum, where a lieutenant-colonel of the Red Army stood side-by-side with top brass of Eastern Command and a senior Cabinet minister, Sir John Anderson. A squadron of British fighter planes circled overhead. Later, in the Regal Cinema, Anderson read a message from Stalin, and then paid tribute. Flags of the United Nations were dipped in salute. The *Cambridge Daily News* said in an editorial:

> No tribute could be more sincere and spontaneous than that which has been paid this weekend to the Red Army . . .

When the Russians' winter campaign drew to a close there was a pause of about three months, broken when the Germans attacked on the Kursk sector on 5th July. Early in August the Russians captured Orel, a vital strategic strongpoint of immense psychological importance because it had been a bastion of the German front since 1941. The Russians took Kharkov on 23rd August and extended their offensive, delivering hammer-blows at widely separated parts of the front one after the other, pushing at each until German resistance stiffened, then holding on there and suddenly switching the main effort to a different point. This produced results. In September the pace of the Russian advances increased, and before the month was out they had reached the River Dnieper, established a series of bridgeheads and, with incredible speed, constructed bridges. At much the same time, further north, on the approach to Moscow, the Germans were forced to abandon Smolensk. By that time they were spread too thinly and had too few reserves effectively to hold their front. So in November the Red Army took Kiev and pressed on at great speed, and Stalin declared "Victory is near".

In fact, however, the Russians were under severe strain throughout the autumn of 1943 on the northern stretch of the front, and repeated Russian offensives failed to crack the line to which the Germans withdrew after evacuating Smolensk. So it was until Christmas Eve, when a new Russian offensive near Kiev swamped the German positions on the first day; soon the Red Army was thrusting boldly forward towards the pre-war frontier with Poland.

Admiration for the Russian effort grew and was unrestrained. The Bishop of

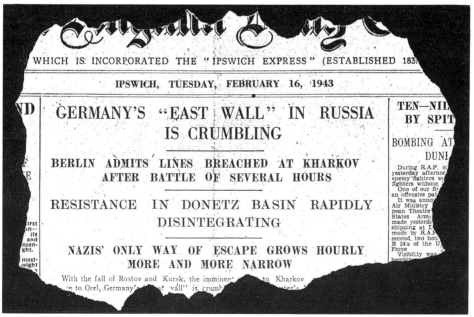

WHICH IS: INCORPORATED THE "IPSWICH EXPRESS" (ESTABLISHED 183

IPSWICH, TUESDAY, FEBRUARY 16, 1943

GERMANY'S "EAST WALL" IN RUSSIA IS CRUMBLING

BERLIN ADMITS LINES BREACHED AT KHARKOV AFTER BATTLE OF SEVERAL HOURS

RESISTANCE IN DONETZ BASIN RAPIDLY DISINTEGRATING

NAZIS' ONLY WAY OF ESCAPE GROWS HOURLY MORE AND MORE NARROW

With the fall of Rostov and Kursk, the imminent ... to Kharkov
... to Orel, Germany's ... wall" is crumb...

TEN—NIL
BY SPIT

BOMBING AT
DUNI

During R.A.F. o
yesterday afternoo
enemy fighters w
fighters without
One of our fig
an offensive pat
It was anno
Air Ministry
pean Theatre
States Army
made yesterd
shipping at I
made by R.A.
second, two hou
B 24's of the U
Force
Visibility was

Chelmsford, Dr Henry Wilson, presiding over a meeting at the Royal Albert Hall, London, on the second anniversary of the German invasion of the USSR, sent this message to his "opposite number in Russia":

> I speak as a Christian bishop to the Christian bishops and Christian people in Russia—a far larger number and percentage of the general population than is the case with the Christian people of this country, "We greet you, we salute you, we thank you, we remember you in our prayers, and we say God bless and God guide the people of Russia and their great leader, Joseph Stalin."

Throughout the year there was a passion for all things Russian, shown in many ways. The BBC broadcast a serialisation of *War and Peace*, and Tolstoy was suddenly a best-seller in Britain, to the extent that copies of his books became unobtainable.

Towards the end of 1943 stories began to filter through of unrest and resistance in the occupied countries of Europe. These *East Anglian Daily Times* headlines were typical:

[19th October] **CIVIL WAR THREAT IN NORTHERN ITALY**

[29th October] **SABOTAGE SWEEPING FRANCE**

[4th November] **NAZIS FEAR REVOLT IN AUSTRIA**

These reports were good for British morale but needed to be treated with reserve, for there were no direct channels of communication through which they could have come. As the year moved to a conclusion, however, there was a new note of confidence in all official statements, never more so than in the communiqué issued after the Allied leaders had met in conference in Teheran. The *East Anglian Daily Times* front page read:

"WE SHALL STRIKE EAST, SOUTH AND WEST"

Allied Leaders' terrible warning to Nazis from Teheran

"NO POWER ON EARTH CAN PREVENT US DESTROYING YOU"

Further to bolster year-end confidence, on Sunday, 26th December the *Scharnhorst*, the pride of the German Navy, was sunk off the coast of Norway by the Royal Navy. And on the last day of the year the *East Anglian Daily Times* reported that 3,000 planes had bombed European targets. Nevertheless, 1943 ended as it had begun, with the biggest, boldest headlines devoted to events on the Eastern Front:

180 MILES BREAK FORCED IN MANSTEIN'S DEFENCES

Russians in five days sweep on 60 miles and
take over a thousand places

Twenty-two German divisions routed

CHAPTER SIX

East Coast Battlefront

BETWEEN the Allied armies in Britain, steadily growing in size and confidence, and the German forces in the Low Countries, unpopular with the local population and apprehensive of attack, lay the coastal plain of Norfolk, Suffolk and Essex and the North Sea. Throughout 1943 this was the battlefront nearest home.

The people who still lived in the eastern counties—there had been large-scale evacuation from the coastal towns—were daily aware of the engines of war. The east coast ports, Great Yarmouth, Lowestoft, Harwich and the smaller havens of the Colne and Blackwater estuary, buzzed with naval vessels that went out to protect merchant convoys, to fight enemy U-boats and coastal craft or to clear (or lay) mines. Lifeboat stations and some of the airfields near the coast were on constant alert for air–sea rescue duties, snatching from the water men whose ships or planes had come to grief. A short distance inland, Army units and Home Guard were deployed to resist an enemy invasion, which during the early months of the year had still not been ruled out.

In 1943 there was a significant amount of shipbuilding in the Colne estuary. The Brightlingsea yard of Aldous Successors Ltd, which had been busily repairing and refitting trawlers, drifters, tugs, motor minesweepers, yachts, MTBs and MGBs and minelayers, built up its labour force to 660 as it expanded its activities to construction of landing craft and bridging pontoons for the invasion fleet. A second Brightlingsea yard, James and Stone, built small vessels of many kinds and modified and repaired landing craft.

Wivenhoe Shipyard, which despite its four-hundred-year tradition of ship-building had fallen derelict by 1939, now employed more than three hundred and its dry dock dealt with a ship a week. It concentrated on minesweepers made entirely of oak and elm grown within twenty-five miles of the yard. A shadow factory was opened at Wivenhoe by Vospers, of Portsmouth, and this employed about 225 on repair of MTBs and other coastal craft.

On the other side of the river at Rowhedge well over three hundred were employed in two yards, one of which built motor minesweepers and the other "austerity" cargo coasters. After a twenty-five-year interval, the Rowhedge Iron Works Company resumed the manufacture of steam engines.

With all this activity there were many tempting targets for the Luftwaffe, and German planes came regularly to attack, though not as frequently or as fiercely as in previous years. Raids on the coastal towns were often by single hit-and-run bombers; such raids came to be regarded almost as routine, attracting headlines only if a plane was brought down or bomb damage was particularly severe. The raiders often came to attack shipping and, finding none, switched their attention to the ports. Occasionally there were bigger raids concentrating on Norwich, Ipswich, Colchester and Chelmsford, and these attacks showed an evident intention to attack specialised targets.

Ships sailing up and down the east coast were marshalled into convoys of forty to fifty vessels; and they constituted the biggest convoy system in the world. London was their focal point. One of the principal cargoes throughout 1943 was coal, with about twenty-five colliers sailing southward every other day from the north-east ports to stock great fuel dumps along the south coast. A two years'

Motor torpedo boats berthed in Felixstowe Dock. Operating from HMS *Beehive*, these 70-foot Vosper MTBs harried German convoys off the Dutch coast while the motor gunboats sought to parry similar forays against British convoys by *Schnellboote* or E-boats.

supply was laid down so that the shipping lanes would not be congested by colliers when the D-Day invasion came and so that the vessels would be available for carrying ammunition and supplies to the invading armies.

The Allied convoys sailed in two parallel lines, stretched out over seven miles. German E-boats came from seawards to attack them, fired ten to sixteen torpedoes, and then headed home. They also mined the channels. It was not easy to protect the convoys, as the official naval historian has explained:

> Only the destroyers and corvettes of the Nore Command and the Rosyth Escort Force, which, week after week and month after month, shepherded these unwieldy convoys, in which some of the masters were as unamenable to convoy discipline as their rusty, salt-caked smoky coasters were incapable of co-ordinated manoeuvres, fully understood and will remember the peculiar problems which the East Coast convoys involved.
>
> Fortunately, the British sailor's gift of humour rose above all the difficulties and dangers, and it may be that the ironic banter often sent over the senior officer's loud-hailer to a particularly stubborn straggler, and the delighted reception accorded to the inevitably abusive retort from the coaster's bridge, did more than the most carefully framed convoy orders and the most courteously conducted convoy conferences to keep these little ships sailing.[1]

At 1st January, 1943, the Nore Command Escort Force consisted of twenty-four destroyers and seven corvettes. The main base for the E-boats they tried to ward off was at Ijmuiden, only ninety miles away. A normal routine for an escort force was to steam out of Great Yarmouth in the late afternoon, test its guns, probably receive the odd air attack, and then pick up a northbound convoy about twenty miles off the coast. After escorting it throughout the night, the force would break off at daylight, enter the Humber, and berth at Immingham. The next day the escort vessels would return with a southbound convoy.

Not all shipping moved in convoy. For example, two Essex sailing barges were lost early in 1943: the *Resolute*, mined off the mouth of the River Crouch in January, and the *Castanet*, which hit a submerged wreck in the River Orwell in February. A third barge, the *Alaric*, of Colchester, was attacked in the Whitaker Channel by six Luftwaffe planes when on passage to Felixstowe on 12th March, and the skipper, Harry James Eves, was killed. His son Adam, who was unscathed, turned the vessel back to Burnham; assistance arrived and the barge, though extensively damaged, was saved.

During the first five months of 1943 only two ships, totalling 6,580 tons, were lost from east coast convoys, but later in the year some big naval battles were fought, one of the biggest on 6th October. It began off Cromer when twenty-eight boats from Ijmuiden attacked convoy FN1160 and were heavily engaged by destroyers and coastal craft of the escort. In a long series of running fights, two enemy vessels were sunk and another damaged, while the only British loss was one trawler which had straggled astern. The laggard was sunk, but the rest of the convoy passed on its way unharmed.

Soon after midnight on 24th October a force of about thirty German E-boats moved to attack another convoy about thirty miles off the east coast, converging in groups on the swept channel from several directions. British destroyers and gunboats foiled the attack, sinking four and damaging seven of the enemy in the course of running fights.

The Navy had many responsibilities. Its minesweepers worked to keep the convoy channel clear. Its Royal Navy Patrol Service boats endeavoured to detect enemy craft before they came within range to attack. Its minelayers sought to deter their approach by putting down an explosive barrier. The gunboats and torpedo boats of its Light Coastal Forces attacked the German E-boats whenever and wherever possible, and that meant regular forays into coastal waters on the other side of the North Sea.

More than sixty minesweepers based at Great Yarmouth were responsible for sweeping the northern section of the channel off the coast from Sheringham light-buoy to the fringe of Lowestoft. Minesweeper flotillas from other ports covered the southern section to the Thames. Late in 1943 many of the trawlers and drifters which had served since 1939 were replaced by new motor minesweepers, designed specially for inshore sweeping. Although during the course of the year Nore Command minesweepers swept 373 ground mines and eighty-six moored mines, their efforts could not be entirely successful, and in November two merchantmen were mined off Harwich.

The Coastal Forces bases were at Great Yarmouth (HMS *Midge*), Lowestoft (HMS *Mantis*), and Felixstowe (HMS *Beehive*). Their operational strength in September, 1943, was: Great Yarmouth, 15 motor torpedo boats (MTBs), 20 motor gunboats (MGBs) and 12 motor launches (MLs); Lowestoft, 8 MTBs, 20 MGBs and 16 MLs; and Felixstowe, 16 MTBs, 7 MGBs and 4 MLs. These were all relatively small vessels.

Whereas the primary offensive armament of the motor torpedo boats was their torpedo tubes and early examples were lightly armed as regards guns, the motor gunboats fairly bristled with guns, carrying a 20-mm Oerlikon aft and four 0.5-inch machine-guns in twin turrets on either side of the bridge. The MGBs were of either 31 or 45 tons, were 70 or 77 feet long, and moved at 40 knots. Coastal Forces craft usually worked in twos and threes rather than as complete flotillas.

At Felixstowe the Light Coastal Forces depot ship HMS *Vulcan*, a converted trawler, and her brood of motor torpedo boats forming the 1st MTB Flotilla operated from the south quay. Elsewhere in the port the 4th and 10th Flotillas were moored. The 21st and 22nd Flotillas of motor gunboats were based at HMS *Mantis* at Lowestoft.

The east coast ports were almost completely in the hands of the Royal Navy, and were hives of activity. Every road approaching the waterfront became a *cul-de-sac*, barred to all but authorised personnel. A description of the unceasing activity has been provided by Captain Peter Dickens, DSO, MBE, DSC, who as a young lieutenant brought his 21st MTB Flotilla to Felixstowe in 1943. One of the huge black hangars which in peacetime had sheltered flying boats and seaplanes had become a maintenance and repair base for the MTBs, and the staff worked all the hours there were:

> Old Lillicrap reigned over the shipwrights in the great hangar along the hard. Our boats could hardly be more up-to-date, yet they were built of wood, as Nelson's had been, and strangely satisfying were the sounds of plane, saw and mallet on chisel, the feel of ankle-deep shavings and sawdust, and the sweet smell of "'onduras me'ogany".[2]

In every department—engineering, electrical, stores and victualling, signals, administration, medical—there was, Captain Dickens found, absolute dedication to the tasks in hand; "and through them all, forming the great majority, was a comely regiment of women"—the WRNS.

> They ran the harbour craft . . . The Wrens coded, sorted and distributed the signals, they cooked and catered . . . In the torpedo shops, Wrens checked pressures and carried out maintenance schedules . . .[3]

They also drove the tractors which moved the boats about the slipways on huge

Wrens driving the tractors that haul a motor torpedo boat from the hangar at Felixstowe in which it has been repaired by "Old Lillicrap" and his shipwrights.

cradles. They worked on the guns and the belts of ammunition, which, after dowsing with salt water, had to be dried and cleaned, oiled and replaced.

> They were fully aware of the significance of that irksome task, as they often showed by being on the jetty when we returned after an action, asking anxiously "Did it work all right?"

When the vessels put to sea it was done with style. Dickens stepped on board precisely at sailing time and ordered "start up".

> Engines came to life not one but all together, shattering Felixstowe Dock with a mighty and bellicose roar. The seagoing boats having previously been moored in the right sequence, with mine on the outside, I would slip, followed by the rest at exactly two lengths interval. A bare 30 yards separated the berth from the point where Tommy Kerr (Captain of *Beehive*) and Ian Trelawney (Staff Officer, Operations) stood to receive our salute, and it was just possible in that space for the crew to get the fenders in, coil down the ropes and fall in smartly on the forecastle. Then the pipe would trill, the men sprang to attention, and the captain saluted . . .[4]

During the early part of 1943 not a great deal was achieved at sea. Some of the boats were not functioning well, and when they were they often made long voyages, with the crews becoming very cold, wet and tired, and returned to harbour without having sighted an enemy craft. Nevertheless there were some lively engagements. Early on 29th March light coastal forces under the command of Lieutenant Donald Goold Bradford intercepted an enemy force off the coast and two motor gunboats engaged five of the E-boats with gunfire. They scored several hits and saw the second boat in the enemy line blow up. One British vessel then rammed the leading E-boat, which heeled over to a 45-degree angle, and part of her stem broke away. Another British boat seriously damaged the fourth boat in the enemy line. Later there was a second attack, in which the last boat in the German line was seriously damaged.

On the same night destroyers on patrol in the same area engaged several other E-boats and scored a number of hits. In these engagements the British forces suffered no casualties and the only damage was that to the vessel which rammed the E-boat. In mid-April there was a rather similar engagement which began in the English Channel and spilled over into the North Sea, off the east coast, in which nine German E-boats and a trawler were hit.

At about this time there were two serious reverses. First, one of the legendary figures of the east coast force, Lieutenant-Commander Robert Hichens, DSO, DSC, senior officer of the 8th MGB Flotilla, was killed in action. He had taken part in 148 operations and fourteen actions before a chance shot ended his career. Known as "Hich" to all who served with the small craft flotillas, he was a modern Drake of the North Sea. Then two days later, during the night of 14th April, the converted Norwegian trawler *Adonis*, master ship of a flotilla of patrol vessels based at Ipswich, was sunk by an E-boat off Lowestoft. (There were two such flotillas at Ipswich, the other master ship being the *Norland*.) Only eleven of a crew

Lieutenant-Commander Robert Hichens, senior officer of the 8th Motor Gunboat Flotilla operating from HMS *Beehive* at Felixstowe, who was killed in action in April.

of thirty-two were saved. Six of those who died had joined the Navy only eight weeks before and were making their first trip to sea[5].

In April the situation began to improve, breakdowns becoming less frequent. Operations were stepped up: the MTBs and MGBs regularly crossed and re-crossed the North Sea, lay all night off the Dutch coast, waiting to attack enemy convoys or returning E-boats, and sometimes penetrated to within a mile or two of the Dutch ports. Still they often returned without having sighted a suitable target, or sometimes a night engagement produced inconclusive results*. It was a business that required patience as well as courage.

At the end of the month Lieutenant Dickens and three of his boats on patrol off Ijmuiden attacked the German 14th Patrol Flotilla, mainly composed of armed trawlers, and torpedoed and sank a small tug of 107 tons. It seemed a small success at the time, but later evidence made plain that the work of the Coastal Forces was at this point making more impact on the German war machine than the crews could have guessed.

During the summer the German E-boats concentrated their attacks on the

*Captain Dickens in his book *Night Action* showed the difficulties of assessing accurately the results of the Coastal Forces' actions. Of one engagement he wrote: "Even with both German and British reports spread out on the desk and several personal recollections to help build the jig-saw, the pieces just will not fit . . ."

Harwich-based patrols. The trawler *Red Gauntlet*, off Harwich with her sweeping gear out early on 5th August, was torpedoed by an E-boat and quickly sank, with heavy casualties. A few weeks later, the ex-Grimsby trawler *Franc Tireur*, also sweeping from Harwich, was torpedoed and sunk with half her crew in an action in which two other trawlers collided; one of those in collision, the *Donna Nook*, foundered. Later again, the former Aberdeen trawler *William Stephen* was torpedoed by an E-boat off Cromer and lost.

As a result of these continued attacks, and because radar cover of the inshore swept channels had improved, the armed trawlers were withdrawn from patrol duty and by October had been replaced by corvettes, which kept watch at night at the danger points. At about the same time there were serious problems with mines, despite all known methods of sweeping—but this was a two-way traffic, for Bomber Command and the Nore Coastal Forces flotillas made frequent sorties to place mines in the enemy's swept channels and harbour entrances.

Felixstowe at this time, like all the coastal towns, was deserted of civilians but full of WRNS, anti-aircraft gun and balloon crews, and coastal defence soldiers. Along the promenade the bathing huts were boarded up, the hotels were empty, there were great rolls and entanglements of barbed wire, steel spikes on the beach, and many warning signs: "Keep out". HMS *Beehive* had taken over a large part of the air station and several hotels and other premises for use as naval billets.

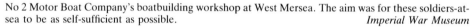

No 2 Motor Boat Company's boatbuilding workshop at West Mersea. The aim was for these soldiers-at-sea to be as self-sufficient as possible.   *Imperial War Museum*

Clacton, where the Light AA Training School was established, housed 8,000 troops, mostly occupying evacuated houses, and the streets were full of Army vehicles.

In each town Servicemen and women formed their special patterns of behaviour and established their own favourite meeting places. In Great Yarmouth, for example, the usual rendezvous for the Coastal Forces officers was the Queen's Hotel, and for the minesweeper officers the Star Hotel. Most sailors, according to Captain Dickens' testimony, preferred to go "out on the town" on their own. Relationships between men and women, he believed, were healthy and uncomplicated:

> I formed the view that the standard war story in which the men were all hopelessly entangled in love affairs at the same time as behaving like heroes was rarely true to life . . . We ran a rugger team . . . Ranting, roaring and pub-bashing were apparently necessary to fulfilment.[6]

Restrictions on the movement of civilians in the coastal belt were tightened up from 1st April, not only in East Anglia but everywhere between the Humber and Penzance, and at some places in South Wales and in Scotland. To a depth of approximately ten miles these were declared "regulated areas", and those who entered were warned that they might meet undefined restrictions, including a complete bar to visiting particular places. Decisions were made by the military authorities, for military purposes, and there was no assurance of any prior notice and no general announcement.

In June, however, other restrictions which had been in force since 1941 were revoked by the Eastern Regional Commissioner. These concerned the mooring, anchoring and keeping of boats in rivers and broads in the region.

From 1st October the Minister of Home Security removed the ban on taking up residence in Hunstanton, Sheringham, Cromer, Mundesley, Caister and a number of other places within ten miles of the east coast. The ban remained in force in respect of Great Yarmouth, Lowestoft, Southwold, Aldeburgh, Felixstowe, Harwich, Frinton and Walton, Clacton, Maldon and Southend.

The biggest problems for the shopkeepers in the coastal towns were caused by the enemy air raids, in which business premises were regularly damaged. There was a good deal of mutual support: in Lowestoft, for example, the traders established a scheme to help those whose premises were wrecked or whose stocks were destroyed, seeking to make available alternative premises, to salvage stocks, or to provide emergency stocks when necessary.

Great Yarmouth was the town where the raids caused most trouble. During 1943 the sirens sounded 217 "alerts" and 97 "crash" alarms (indicating imminent danger), but only seven raids actually developed. Seventy-two people were killed and 124 injured[7].

One of the worst experiences was on 18th March when a Dornier Do.217 sneak raider came in from the North Sea just before dawn, circled and swept low

The WRNS quarters in Queens Road, Yarmouth, after the air raid of 18th March. Thirteen girls died in the attack, but thirteen others were rescued alive from the rubble.

over the town from the landward side. It dropped seven high-explosive bombs across the southern part of the town, one of which hit a group of large houses at the junction of Queens Road and Nelson Road. One was a WRNS hostel; it was completely demolished, fire broke out in the debris, and though rescue workers made valiant efforts thirteen girls were killed and about twelve others seriously injured. Thirteen were brought alive from the rubble under which they were buried. In this raid, too, a laundry in the southern part of the borough received a direct hit, and two churches and over five hundred houses were damaged.

This was a harrowing day for Great Yarmouth, for the Luftwaffe returned shortly before midnight and, despite an hour-long artillery barrage put up by the ground defences, dropped four parachute mines: one at the south end of the Fishwharf, one on maltings at Southtown, and two on the marshes west of Caister Road which caused blast damage to Smith's potato crisp factory and other premises.

Great Yarmouth faced a new form of terror on 7th May, when the German Focke-Wulf FW.190 fighter-bombers appeared for the first time. Their technique was to dive wing tip to wing tip and then fan out, dropping high-explosive bombs from such low altitudes that they often appeared to be travelling horizontally and frequently went through obstacles or struck the ground and bounced up again over the tops of houses before exploding.

The first of these raids occurred in daylight. Damage was widespread, especially in the shopping centre. Vauxhall station was blasted; one bomb, before it exploded in the road outside, passed right through two passenger coaches and severed both sets of rails some distance outside the station. Another bomb behaved rather similarly at Southtown station, passing through a malthouse, the station building and a passenger coach before coming to rest in the middle of the track beside a platform; it failed to explode. A naval bomb disposal officer who was waiting to catch the train immediately jumped down and defused the bomb! Thirteen people were killed and fifty-one injured in this short, sharp tip-and-run raid.

Four days later Great Yarmouth suffered grievously again when at about 8.45 am, when the streets were crowded with people going to work, twenty-eight FW.190s sneaked in from a sea haze, flying very low with a strong sun behind them. Half of them attacked patrol boats, the other half concentrated on a residential area in the northern part of the town, where they dropped fourteen high-explosive bombs. A party of about thirty ATS girls had just marched briskly to their billet in the morning sunshine; five minutes after they entered the billet it was razed to the ground by a direct hit and twelve girls were killed. Thirty-seven other people died and forty-one were injured that day in many other wrecked homes. One of the raiders was brought down by AA fire and another by an RAF Mustang. The raid was all over within a few minutes.

Lowestoft also had its worst raid of the year in May, and also at the hands of FW.190 fighter-bombers. Just before dusk on 12th May about a dozen of them swept over the town just above roof level and machine-gunned the streets. One bomb completely demolished a public house. Rescue workers toiled all night, but there was no-one to bring out alive; about a dozen died in the pub, and in total seventeen civilians and fourteen servicemen lost their lives and over a hundred people were injured. A number of houses were completely destroyed and hundreds were damaged by blast. Again, the raid was all over in a few minutes.

Other coastal towns were targeted from time to time and most major towns just inland from the coast were occasionally raided during this period. Norwich was visited by a lone Dornier Do.217 during the afternoon of New Year's Day. It made a rooftop-level attack, dropping a string of nine 50-kg bombs on a congested area of small houses in which a few people were slightly injured.

Chelmsford suffered three attacks at monthly intervals, the first on 12th March. The second was soon after midnight on 15th April, when considerable damage was done by about 2,500 incendiaries, nineteen high-explosive bombs and two parachute mines which dropped on the town. At the prison the governor's house and a block of stores were gutted by fire and two warders' houses were burned down. Good conduct prisoners joined the firemen fighting the blaze; with twenty-five appliances it took five hours to extinguish it. The county offices and several factories, including a suet factory, were damaged, but there were no deaths and only one severe injury. The third raid, in the early hours of 14th May, concentrated on the Marconi factory and succeeded in disrupting production there for nearly a month.

The defence forces put up a heavy anti-aircraft barrage, and the Germans later admitted the loss of four planes. One of them, a Junkers Ju.88, landed in a field of oats. The crash woke a farm worker living close by, Mr George P. Ranson, who hurriedly dressed and went out and found four airmen near the plane, two of them lying wounded in a ditch. Afterwards he related:

> I stuck my fingers out as if I had a revolver, and up went the first Nazi's hands. I undid his belt and took his revolver. Some soldiers and two local members of the Home Guard, both in uniform, one carrying his rifle and bayonet, arrived and the work of disarming the Nazis was completed.

Ipswich was hit at dawn on 2nd June by FW.190s, part of a force which had intended to bomb Harwich but was thwarted by the balloon barrage there. The other part diverted to attack Felixstowe. Eleven people were killed. The FW.190

NAZI AIRMEN CAPTURED: Mr. Geo. Ranson, a farm worker, who was first on the scene when a Junkers 88 crashed in East Anglia. In the semi-darkness he challenged the four enemy airmen, pretending he had a revolver by thrusting out his hand, and the leading Nazi promptly threw up his hands in surrender. (E.A.D.T. photo.)

YOU MUST COLLECT YOUR RATION BOOKS

Farmworker Mr George Ranson, who captured four German airmen whose Junkers Ju.88 crashed near his Essex home. *East Anglian Daily Times* fighter-bombers had presented a challenge to AA Command because of the suddenness and brevity of their attacks—the average time of engagement for the light AA guns was only six seconds. Great Yarmouth was provided with barrage balloons, other defensive techniques were introduced, and the attacks ceased; that on Ipswich was the last.

Hundreds of people over a wide area who had been sickened by these vicious hit-and-run raids found an opportunity to vent their emotions on 20th April, when an aerial battle developed over the sea off Clacton. A formation of Luftwaffe planes flew very high over the town, and when well out to sea one was seen to go into a steep dive, with an RAF Spitfire on its tail. There was a burst of machine-gun fire, the bomber fell in flames, and many of the spectators shouted and clapped.

Enemy aerial activity slackened during the summer and autumn. During the night of 23rd/24th October about thirty planes arrived over Lowestoft shortly before midnight and unloaded high explosives and incendiaries, but most fell on marshland north of the town. The nurses' home at the Poor Law Institution at Oulton was gutted and about a hundred nearby houses damaged.

There was a sharp attack on Ipswich during the evening of 3rd November, when bombs were scattered widely. Several people were killed, All Hallows' Church and a nursing home were hit, a number of fires were started, and damage to houses made nearly two hundred homeless. On the same day nine people were killed when there was a direct hit on a shelter in the village of Rushmere St Andrew; sixty houses were destroyed and a hundred damaged at Bramford; a big fire was started at the chemical works of Fison, Packard and Prentice there; and bombs also fell on Yoxford and Eyke.

There were a number of minor raids during November and December, including one on 10th December in which four HE bombs were dropped in Castle Park at Colchester, causing four casualties.

Throughout the year the Luftwaffe attempted to bomb the East Anglian airfields from which the Allied bombing offensive against the enemy was being conducted, but without inflicting serious damage. Another consequence of that offensive was the added responsibilities put upon the east coast lifeboat crews and the RAF air–sea rescue units. The latter operated initially only from Martlesham Heath, but as the Allied bombing campaign developed they were extended to Coltishall, Horsham St Faiths and Bircham Newton. Lysander and Walrus rescue planes worked in close liaison with 63-foot air–sea rescue launches based at Wells, Gorleston, Felixstowe and elsewhere. To aid the search aircraft, crews who "ditched" wore yellow lifejackets and skullcaps and they were provided with fluorescein, which could colour the sea a yellowish green, and with smoke signals. Special rescue floats were also positioned off the coast in areas where aerial combats took place frequently; they were painted bright yellow and red and carried clothing, food and water, a primus stove, and signalling apparatus. When damaged bombers were limping home the lifeboatmen were frequently called on to stand by, ready to help if pilots failed to make landfall. Crews mustered at their stations and sat talking or playing cards until they were required to go into action or given the stand-down. This happened to the Walton crew seventeen times in a single month.

Lifeboats had also on occasions to help naval vessels. Landing craft being assembled on the east coast in preparation for the planned invasion of Europe sometimes found themselves in trouble. The lifeboat *J. B. Proudfoot* at Southend was called out in August and again in December to tow in landing craft. The Navy also had need of the lifeboat on the last day of January when a firefloat based at Southend, the *Gladys*, crashed into the pier in a storm and threatened to cut it in two. The Naval Control Service, which directed the North Sea convoys, had its headquarters at the end of the pier and would have been seriously inconvenienced if the pier had been severed. One of the lifeboat crew bravely dropped from the pier on to the pitching deck of *Gladys* and secured a line from the lifeboat so that the firefloat could be towed off, taken under the lee of the pier, and handed over to the Naval Control.

Apart from these more unusual duties, lifeboatmen maintained their customary service to shipping in distress. The Clacton lifeboat *Edward Z. Dresden* went out twice during the year to barges carrying brick rubble to Maldon. On 6th April the barge *Tam o'Shanter*, with only the skipper and a boy on board, was in distress. When the lifeboat reached her the skipper refused to abandon his vessel and requested a tow to Brightlingsea, but the towline parted and both vessels anchored for the night to await more favourable conditions. Next morning, in a strong westerly gale with a heavy sea, a second attempt at towing was thwarted, so the barge made sail for Harwich, with the lifeboat accompanying. Suddenly it took on a great deal of water and capsized, throwing into the sea the skipper, the boy and three lifeboatmen who had gone on board. Two of the lifeboatmen were picked up; the others lost their lives.

One East Anglian sailor returned home during 1943 with a story more remarkable than all these dramas and excitements of maritime life in East Anglia. He was Albert Horlock, of Brook Street, Manningtree, who returned on leave in February after two and a half years at sea. Several days out from a South American port his ship was torpedoed during the night, and sank in bad weather. After swimming for some time he was picked up and spent six days in an open boat with sixty other people, some of them women and children, before being rescued by a Vichy French cruiser and taken to Casablanca, where they were interned. The morning after torpedoing the vessel the German U-boat surfaced and came alongside the survivors' open boat. The commander, speaking perfect English, explained that he had been educated at Oxford and knew England well. He promised to radio for assistance, and took some of the women and children on board the submarine and gave them hot meals; some stayed on the enemy vessel for two or three days.

CHAPTER SEVEN

Squeezing Out the Last Ounce

AFTER well over three years of war, the scale of Britain's national effort was prodigious. Men and women had been conscripted or cajoled into every kind of essential activity to the point where little more seemed possible. Every available acre of land had been ploughed to produce more food. Factories worked day and night. Non-essential goods were no longer produced, and the staples of life—food, clothing, fuel—were severely rationed. All this had been necessary to ensure survival during the dark days when the Germans had set the pace and exerted the pressure.

But a new phase had begun. Fighting now with powerful Allies—Russia and the United States—Britain was confident of victory ahead and was preparing for the final assault to achieve it: an invasion of mainland Europe. That was an enterprise requiring the very last ounce to be squeezed from the reservoir of national resources and energy.

On the last day of 1942 the Minister of Labour, Mr Ernest Bevin, remarked that "the task of mobilising the man and woman-power of the nation has been no easy one. We have had to place a great deal of strain on the whole population, but the way the British people have responded has been such that it amazes the whole world." He knew, though he did not say so at that time, that the screw was going to be turned much tighter. The Service chiefs had revised their manpower requirements. The Army needed 250,000 more men, and the RAF 120,000, over and above the figures sanctioned for 1942.

The King signed a proclamation on 13th January lowering the age at which women were liable to be conscripted from twenty to nineteen. Single women aged nineteen were to be called up immediately but given an option to become nurses or to work in the factories as alternatives to joining the Services. With this proclamation, the situation was that all men were called up immediately they reached their eighteenth birthday and all women on their nineteenth birthday. On 29th January Mr Bevin announced in the Commons that all women between the ages of eighteen and forty-five, except those with children under fourteen living with them, were liable to be directed into part-time work.

In East Anglia the emphasis was on farm labour. When the Minister of Agriculture, Mr R. S. Hudson, set farmers new production targets for 1943, calling for an additional 750,000 acres under tillage, he warned that the Army would be unable to help with the harvest (as it had done the previous year, when 80,000 soldiers had worked in the fields) and that farmers would have to look to the Women's Land Army, to part-timers, and to Italian prisoners-of-war. There was a promise that War Agricultural Executive Committees would open more hostels for the Women's Land Army and would organise auxiliary labour in the form of Irish immigrants and Italian prisoners-of-war, but the Minister thought half a million part-timers would be necessary over the period from spring to late autumn. Townsfolk would have to come into the country to lend a hand.

The expansion of the Women's Land Army proceeded rapidly. By the end of March it was 58,221 strong—almost doubled in a year—and over a thousand girls and women were joining every week. But still a deep conservatism affected East Anglian farmers, and many were slow to recruit women and loath to accept Italian prisoners-of-war, despite the blandishments of the county Agricultural Executive Committees. The West Suffolk committee announced at the end of April that it had reports from employers showing how satisfactory the prisoners-of-war were as workers, but the "between-the-lines" message was that the committee wanted a lot more Italians to be recruited. It was agreed that those with good conduct records might be billeted with the farmers who employed them, living in the farmhouse or in the homes of farm employees, or even lodged in a barn or outhouse on the farm "provided it is healthy, warm and comfortable".

Farmers had to accept responsibility for custody of the prisoners-of-war and had to see that certain security conditions were met, but the military authorities visited regularly to keep an eye on things. Farmers paid the WAEC forty shillings a week for the services of each prisoner for the first three months, forty-eight shillings a week thereafter, and they were repaid twenty-one shillings for providing full board and lodging. The Italians were paid for overtime work at the rate of one shilling an hour, rising to 1s 3d after the first three months, but no payment was made by the farmers directly to the prisoners—they had to be paid by the War Office, in accordance with the Geneva Convention.

Meanwhile, farmers encouraged their regular workers to stay on well after the normal retirement age. At the Westley Hall Estate farm, near Bury St Edmunds, the labour force in 1943 included two brothers, Thomas and Robert Goldsmith, who were eighty-one and seventy-nine years old respectively, and both of whom had been employed on that farm since they were ten. They had followed their father, who had worked there for over fifty years.

At the other end of the age scale, heads of all secondary and public schools were asked by the government to organise parties to work on the farms in term-time and to move into special harvest camps, supervised by teachers and others, during the holidays. At least 50,000 schoolchildren were called for, and an all-in wage of eightpence an hour was offered to boys and girls between the ages of fourteen and nineteen. The response was good; West Suffolk County School, for example, undertook to do 10,000 hours of farm work during the Easter holidays.

There were many successful school camps during the harvest. An example in Suffolk was that at Bachelors Farm, Hundon, organised jointly by the WAEC and the Suffolk Boy Scouts' Association, which housed under canvas 150 to 180 boys at

A newspaper advertisement issued by the Ministry of Agriculture and Fisheries at the beginning of the year. *East Anglian Daily Times*

a time and was maintained for six weeks, during which time it completed 40,000 work-hours. The boys rose at 7 am and after breakfast were taken in parties to farms over a fifteen-mile radius. They took packed lunches and returned to camp by 6.30 pm for hot dinners served in a big marquee, and then there was a camp fire and sing-song before they turned in. Weekends were devoted to Scouting activities.

The farmers' sex prejudice was not yet eradicated, for the headmistress of the Ipswich Northgate School for Girls commented:

> It is unfortunate, but the farmers of Suffolk seem to be frightened of schoolgirls. Once they have seen the work they can do they are eager to employ them, but the number of farmers who can be persuaded to give them a trial is limited.

Land girls were better appreciated, however, and by the end of the year "Lavengro", the *East Anglian Daily Times* agricultural correspondent, who had always been sceptical of their value, was changing his tune:

> Compared with the time when they were at first available, a very different opinion is now held about members of the Women's Land Army in general by those who have had the advantage of their help. While it is true some have not been a success, and have consequently been required to take up other war work, taking the Land Girls as a whole they have been most useful. Tributes to their competency and enthusiasm in their new jobs have been given by not a few of my farming friends.

Sunday, 4th July was designated "Farm Sunday". The Duchess of Gloucester visited Cambridge to present good service awards to members of the Women's

IPSWICH: Lord Woolton, with Lady Woolton, Lady Cranworth, the Lord-Lieutenant of Suffolk (Lord Stradbroke) and the Countess of Stradbroke, photographed on Saturday on the occasion of the Food Minister's visit to the town to speak at the Women's Land Army Rally at the Public Hall.
(E.A.D.T. Photo.)

Lord Woolton visited Ipswich in July to address a Women's Land Army rally. There were by that time some 6,600 land girls in the eastern counties. *East Anglian Daily Times*

Land Army from Cambridgeshire, Huntingdonshire and the Isle of Ely, three hundred of whom paraded from Parker's Piece to the Guildhall. A fortnight later Lord Woolton visited Ipswich, and the march-past of hundreds of land girls in their green sweaters and khaki breeches was such a sight as the town had never seen before. It was announced that East Suffolk at that point had nearly 1,100 land girls, West Suffolk had 635, Norfolk 1,369, and Essex 3,536. The national total, by this date, had reached 69,400.

Large numbers of volunteer adults came forward. In Ipswich, bus-loads left the car park every night during July, supplemented in August by secondary school boys and high school girls. The Ipswich Land Club, which supervised the operation, found 3,100 farm jobs for them. Fruit-picking camps for holiday makers were organised by the Norfolk WAEC, the first in July at Westwick Fruit Farm, Worstead, where accommodation was provided for a hundred men and women, and others soon after at Emneth, Terrington St John and Upwell, near King's Lynn. These camps continued until the end of September, and people came from all over Britain, including some Commonwealth troops on leave.

A relentless campaign to increase the national force of voluntary workers was maintained all summer; during June public meetings and rallies took place to recruit part-timers in every principal town in the region. Already at that stage it was estimated that a million women were giving voluntary unpaid service.

Three million more were employed; nine out of every ten single women, and eight out of ten married women, were in the forces or in industry. The government had to accept that "Great Britain had reached the limits of mobilisation"[1]. From August the call-up was speeded up. Girls of eighteen and a half were required to register on 21st August so that they could be called up immediately they were nineteen.

Then came an announcement which shook the nation: women aged between forty-seven and fifty were required to register during September and October. Parliament and Press registered strong misgivings about the idea of conscripting grandmothers. The Ministry of Labour, knowing it was treading on delicate ground, declared that the matter would be handled "with the very greatest care", and added: "There is no intention of sending this type of relatively older women all over the country. In the main, they will be regarded as immobile."

Women were already living under immense pressures. Mrs Elspeth House, who lived at Elsworth, near Cambridge, committed to paper an account of her working routine:

> Digging up the kitchen garden has taken up all my spare time during the past two weeks ... For the last two months I have been working part-time at Papworth Industries, doing metal work, riveting, etc, all repair work to Stirling wings and fins, 8.30 to 1 pm, Mondays to Fridays. I also run this house, as before. I had three land girls billeted—now have only one.[2]

She woke at 6 am each day and left her home at 7.55 to cycle three and a half miles to the factory, where her work consisted of drilling out old rivets. They had a ten-minute break, from 9.50 to 10 am. After this working day, she turned out in the evening for a Women's Institute meeting.

Some women found factory work uncongenial, as a Bury St Edmunds diarist, Miss Winifred Last, noted:

> I hear that lots of our country girls sent into the factories get a sort of nervous breakdown through fright. Nobody at the Shirehall wants to go into factories ...

Others found genuine interest and satisfaction in their duties. Enthusiastic or resentful, dedicated or resigned, most women had no option but to leave their homes and do as the government told them. The screw was tightened weekly.

By October boys and girls who had reached the age of sixteen were required to report at Ministry of Labour offices, ostensibly so that they could be issued with new, adult national registration cards. But at the same time particulars of each one were noted and afterwards forwarded to local education authorities, which then interviewed and sought to enrol those who had failed to join any youth organisations.

The government decided to tighten the rules on the deferment of call-up of arts students. At Cambridge a Jesus man pointed out that:

> Those who have hitherto been allowed to come up have received during their brief period of residence a fairly intensive military training, so that their time at university has been by no means wasted, even from a strictly military point of view.

When the new term began in October the 2,700 undergraduates in residence matched the number a year earlier, but a large proportion of them were "short course" entrants whose average length of residence was to be four terms.

A new Fire Guard scheme was introduced, making liable for duty all men aged eighteen to sixty-three and all women aged twenty to forty-five, if they were not already serving in some other way. This extended the age limit for men from sixty to sixty-three and was designed "to rope in all dodgers", but the announcement said it would result in "minimum demands on women".

Mobilising labour is one thing, getting the best results another, and not everyone worked conscientiously. During February, 1943, Mass Observation

Women who found themselves in the services had to endure the same discipline as their male comrades. This photograph of a WAAF billet inspection at RAF Feltwell was taken in July, 1943.
Imperial War Museum

invited its regular correspondents to describe a typical working day. This account by an eighteen-year-old laboratory chemist working in Ipswich is illuminating:

> Mother called me at 7.45. She had overslept, so I did not get my usual cup of tea in bed . . . I cycled to work (this takes about three minutes) and arrived there at 8.15—instead of 8. I am the only one who starts at 8 in the physical testing laboratory, so, as usual, I was alone for the first hour. A friend who works in the nearby machine shop came in soon after I arrived. He wanted some plywood. I went into the "chemi-lab", borrowed an empty case and broke it up for him. We chatted until 9, when George, "the boy", came in, swept up and cleaned the machines.
>
> I then went into the "chemi-lab" again and made some nitrogen iodide (when dry this explodes at a touch). I took some over to the office block and sprinkled it on the passage floor to dry out. This was a joke I had been planning for some days. About half an hour later there was a phone call from the office. A female voice said: "Will you come and clear up whatever it was you put over here?" I feigned ignorance and rang off.
>
> At 9.20 the chief inspector arrived and, after his usual remarks about the weather, his indigestion and his car, sat down with the *Daily Mail*.
>
> I went over to the office block to reconnoitre. The typists had discovered that the stuff could be exploded by scraping the floor with their feet. This they were doing, screaming with delight at each little bang. They accosted me and asked me what it was—said they wanted to take some to a dance. I muttered something about "secret formula" and hurriedly left.
>
> Back in the test room, I did some tensile tests until 10.30, when I lunched—Marmite sandwiches. Afterwards I sat for a while looking through catalogues of gramophone records. Then a yarn in the "chemi-lab", more yarns in the machine shop, then at 12.45 home to dinner. During my dinner hour, apart from eating (potato pie, greens, sponge pudding), I glanced through father's *Daily Herald*, played Sibelius' *Karelia Suite* on my gram, and read a chapter of *Maradick at Forty*, by Hugh Walpole. Back to work at 2 pm.
>
> Until 4 I worked fairly steadily—pulling tensile tests, graphing and writing certificates. At 4 the chief went off to the canteen for tea and my friend from the machine shop came in. We discussed making some ultra-modern stools from tubular bronze—I don't expect this to ever get beyond discussion. A little more browsing in a record catalogue passed the time until 5.30 pm. I had tea in the works canteen—Welsh rarebit, bread and butter, cake and tea (6d). I left about 6.30 and went to see the film *In This Our Life*. I returned home by 11 pm—supper and bed.[3]

East Anglia had more farms than factories, and it was there that the really stupendous production feats were achieved. As 1943 began, the farming columnist of the *East Anglian Daily Times*, "Lavengro", summed up:

> Before the war not enough food was raised in this country to feed the population for more than three days a week, if that. Last year British farmers provided enough to feed the nation 4½ days in every week, and this year sufficient must come from the land to feed the population of these islands 6½ days a week.

The year began well. Sheep farmers said they could never remember a better lambing time. The weather was ideal for getting on with work on the land, as an exceptionally mild winter ended with a dry February and a sunny March. By May the Minister was able to announce that the pre-war acreage of wheat had been doubled. Norfolk farmers were asked to grow 5,000 acres of flax, but their main

BRITAIN'S PERFECT VILLAGE GREEN GOES TO WAR: Britain's largest village green—at Great Bentley, in Essex—sometimes called "Britain's perfect village green," is being ploughed. Potatoes will be planted in its 50 acres. For centuries the villagers, who to-day number 1,300, had had grazing rights to the green. For centuries this turf had been theirs—for their pleasures and their pastures. One man who has his bitter regrets is the oldest of them all, Mr. J. H. Sizer, who is 90. Mr. Sizer remembers volunteers after the Crimea War drilling on the green. Photo shows: Mr. Sizer talking to George Bennett, aged 18, who is ploughing the green. (Photo: Topical Press.)

The ploughing of Great Bentley green was a matter of regret for older inhabitants such as ninety-year-old Mr J. H. Sizer, who was photographed talking to eighteen-year-old tractor driver George Bennett.
East Anglian Daily Times

crop was barley for malting purposes. They declared themselves unhappy with the price fixed, but conceded that barley was a better financial proposition than oats or wheat.

The Minister of Agriculture was unhappy because Norfolk farmers had been putting too much land down to grass, and he wrote to the WAEC pointing out that as a result the acreage available for crops for direct human consumption had been smaller in the 1942 harvest than in 1941. Planting leys might be excellent farming, but it reduced immediate output, and the Minister gave instructions that no farmer was to lay down more than one-eighth of his arable land to the one-year leys in any one year, and no leys of longer than one year's duration.

This policy upset the farmers, who argued that some of the ploughed-up grassland had produced four cereal crops in succession, and this could not be repeated. They had no choice but to fall into line, however, and at the end of the year the Minister explained that he had planned for a crisis harvest, with the maximum area at all costs:

> When I said "at all costs" I meant it. We had to take risks, risks of some drain on the fertility of our land, risks of a smaller cropped area in 1944, or of smaller yields.

In East Suffolk, according to the chairman of its War Agricultural Executive Committee, Mr Stuart Paul, practically every acre of derelict land had been brought under cultivation by June. Thousands of acres had been moled and tile drained, and hundreds of miles of ditches cleaned out.

Very little land anywhere escaped the plough. Even on many operational airfields food crops were grown, and RAF staff helped harvest them in their spare time. The fifty-acre village green at Great Bentley, reputedly the largest in Britain, was ploughed and planted with potatoes. On the royal estate at Sandringham 539 acres had been ploughed since the outbreak of war, to give a total of 977 acres of arable. The King's private golf course was growing oats and rye, and six acres of lawn in front of the house were under rye. Beetroot and parsnips grew in what had been ornamental flower beds. Naturally, Sandringham farming made use of all the latest developments, and when the King and Queen, with the two princesses, inspected the work in hand during August photographs in the press showed them watching a combine harvester, which was followed by a mechanical straw baler hauled by a tractor driven by one of the fourteen land girls employed on the estate.

The weather continued to be kind. A sample of new winter oats was offered at Ipswich Corn Hall on 20th June, cut and threshed with a combine the previous day. At Kitchen Farm, Bulmer, they started cutting King George wheat on 17th July and the farmer, Mr H. W. Cardy, reported that to be the earliest for wheat in that

The arrival of combine harvesters on Suffolk farms was news. This one was pictured "cutting, threshing and bagging on a field of barley at Bridge Farm, Wickham Market". *East Anglian Daily Times*

district within living memory, by a fortnight. "Lavengro" wrote in the *East Anglian Daily Times* on 24th July:

> This year's harvest is one of the earliest on record . . . Farmers of long standing have no recollection of cutting wheat at so early a date as the middle of July. A considerable acreage of corn has fallen to the binder this week in most parts of Suffolk and in Essex.

There was almost an euphoric note to reports from the countryside. On 27th July the *East Anglian Daily Times* stated that harvesting of corn was under way on farms all over the southern half of England, and volunteer workers had filled the farm camps. Because of the spring drought, yields might not be up to average in some of the eastern counties, but the twenty-five per cent increase in the wheat acreage meant that it should still be a record harvest. Harvest conditions in August were ideal for combines, and they played a larger part than ever before in clearing the fields. Their value was now recognised by all but the most blinkered farmers, and the Ministry promised their number would be substantially increased in time for the 1944 harvest. Driers were still something of a novelty, but the Ministry said that considerable numbers would be manufactured in Britain so that they could be widely used in 1944. By the end of August the maltsters had bought all the barley they needed, and "Pightle" reported:

> On many farms this week has brought a finish to harvesting operations, probably the earliest and easiest for many years. But failure of many crops sown for autumn and winter keep makes it imperative to plant a large acreage of quick-growing seeds to try to bridge the gap before next summer.

The intensity of farming effort certainly increased during 1943, but so did the strength of feeling of East Anglian farmers against Whitehall and Westminster. The main grumble was about the government-fixed farm prices. Back in November, 1940, the Minister of Agriculture had said: "Prices will be subject to adjustment to the extent of any substantial change in the costs of production." Farmers believed that this was a pledge and that it had not been honoured, especially as regards the increased costs of wages. The fixing of wages had been taken out of the hands of county committees late in 1942 and made the responsibility of a Central Agricultural Wages Board. In the new year the National Union of Agricultural Workers asked for a one-pound increase for men, to establish a new minimum of £4 a week, and a five shillings increase for women, to bring them to £2 8s, and a working week of forty-eight hours. The Central Wages Board proposed £3 5s for men and £2 5s for women, and invited the views of county committees.

This consultation procedure ended in July with the announcement of a farmworkers' "charter", the main provisions of which were: no change in the men's national minimum wage of £3 for a week not exceeding fifty-two hours during the eight summer months and forty-eight hours during the rest of the year; overtime at 1s 5d per hour on weekdays and 1s 9d at weekends and on public holidays; a minimum of £2 5s for women over eighteen for a week not exceeding fifty hours summer and forty-eight hours winter; and a minimum four days' holiday a year. The farmworkers' union announced that it would immediately lodge a renewed claim for £4 a week. Leaders of the union showed remarkable restraint. At the annual conference of the Norfolk branch at Norwich on 3rd July the national president, Mr E. G. Gooch, said:

> The agricultural industry is almost unique in that there have been no strikes, no absenteeism. We are cheered by the war news and the turn in the tide, and encouraged by the stirring lead of our wonderful prime minister. The farmworkers will continue working towards an end—speedy victory for the United Nations, and life, liberty and human happiness.

The conference passed a resolution expressing similar sentiments, but one of its national officers, Mr A. C. Dann, complained that "cattle were often better housed than the farmworkers" and served notice that when the war ended they would look to be well fed, housed, shod and educated.

After the issue of wages had been settled, the announcement of new farm prices was a long time coming. Mr Hudson announced them in November, claiming that in a full year they would leave farmers rather better off than they were already. The price for milk was increased a penny; the average total return to growers of wheat, rye, oats and sugar beet was to be maintained at the same level; but the maximum price of barley was to be reduced. The manner in which the price levels were fixed meant that the small farmer should benefit at the expense of the big man, according to the Minister. East Anglian farmers disagreed strongly.

They seem to have got wind of the Minister's policy before he made the announcement. A large turn-out of West Suffolk farmers at Bury St Edmunds the day before resolved that farmers were "staggered to learn that there was any suggestion by the government that the price of any single commodity should be reduced". The protest motion recalled the November, 1940, pledge. The Executive of the Suffolk NFU met in Ipswich on 31st November and the chairman, Mr Makens Turner, declared that the new prices would mean a deficit for many farmers, a substantial one in many cases. According to "Lavengro", writing in the *East Anglian Daily Times*, the average Suffolk farmer was likely to be £400 a year worse off. He asserted that they would have no more negotiations with the Minister or his staff in relation to prices, War Committee work, or wages until he had apologised for his "insult".

Mr Hudson, despite the breaking storm of farmers' anger, stood his ground. And he had this to say about his 1940 "pledge":

> The government, when it settled the wording, knew what it had in mind, and the meaning was explained to the farmers' leaders in the spring of 1942 during price negotiations. They were told that the pledge had been given to the farming community as a whole, and had been related to the whole range of products to which the fixed prices extended. It did not mean that the price of each and every agricultural product would be raised in proportion to increases in the cost of producing that commodity.

The East Anglian farmers erupted more fiercely. Mr Hollis Clayton, chairman of the Essex NFU, declared "We are straightforward, honest people and we have no use for people or a government who cannot stand up to their word." A meeting of the Essex Executive in Chelmsford on 10th December resolved:

> Since Mr R. S. Hudson is doing such a disservice to the farming industry and to the nation by his dishonest presentation of the farm prices situation to the public and by his failure to honour the pledges he had given to the farming industry, this branch demands his resignation and his replacement by one upon whose word farmers can rely and who is capable of reasonable negotiation with farmers' representatives.

Soon it became known that fifty of the fifty-nine NFU branches in Britain had protested against the government's price proposals. The general tenor of the protests was that Mr Hudson—and many other people—simply did not understand the realities of life on the farms. Mr Alfred Lewis, chairman of Norfolk NFU, said "I do not think the general public realise the large extent to which the light lands depend on a good price for barley to recoup losses on other crops . . . It was only because of high prices for barley that we readily undertook to grow on unsuitable land a much larger acreage of wheat."

There was no doubt that many of the public discounted the farmers' grumbles and felt they were earning good money. Miss Last noted in her diary:

> Last time I was at Sudbury, Mr K——, the Relieving Officer, was saying that in the last three years his son had earned more in farming than he himself did in a lifetime. He said he kept afloat during the bad years before the war by becoming Relieving Officer, as well as farmer.[4]

Whitehall contrived to upset farmers in other ways, too, and as always "Lavengro" was quick to voice their resentment. The Ministry of Information, he reported, was sending out young women "to pester farmers with inane questions". The questions included: *Why did you become a farmer? What was your father's occupation? How many children have you? What are their ages? How are they being educated?* and *What newspapers do you read?* The matter was raised in Parliament, where the Minister of Information said that twelve people had been employed for five weeks on this survey in East Anglia, and twenty-five in the country as a whole. The Ministry of Agriculture justified the exercise with this explanation: "If we can discover the educational standards and the interests of the men to whom we are appealing, we can prepare our own literature and campaigns to suit."

There was one way in which farmers were able to combine their business with a measure of relaxation, and that was at the horse sales. Many in East Anglia were still better disposed towards horses than towards farm machinery, and the Suffolk Horse Society's spring sale was extended to two days in February; as the *East Anglian Daily Times* explained, "the increasing use of good horses on the land has led to owners of Suffolk Punches breeding more of them".

Again at Woodbridge Horse Show on Easter Monday there was a record

"Make do and mend" was the order of the day, and advertisements such as this were to be seen in the region's newspapers.
Cambridge Local Collection

wartime entry of animals, and the Suffolk Horse Society's two-day summer sale at Ipswich set further records. In September there was a third sale of Suffolk horses at Ipswich. Taking all three shows together, 696 horses changed hands for a total of £84,622.

The food position remained difficult during 1943. The year began with cuts in the cheese ration—first from eight to six ounces per person per week, within four weeks to four ounces, and from the beginning of May to three ounces. There was just one egg per person per week during January, and during that month an "Eat less Bread" campaign was launched. A scheme for rationing bread had been prepared, but voluntary restraint proved sufficient. Hotels and restaurants were asked not to serve rolls and toast at lunches and dinners, except on request, and then only small pieces, and not to place butter on tables, as that would encourage requests for bread. They were urged to offer large portions of potatoes and other available vegetables. In March the Food Ministry decreed that twopence-worth of the 1s 2d weekly meat ration must be taken in the form of canned corn beef. The only bright spot was that the ration of chocolate and sweets was maintained at three ounces a week.

The quest for enough to eat wearied many housewives. Mrs Sarah Williams, in Sheringham, constantly complained to her diary after her shopping expeditions:

January 20th: One has to shop every single day now. There is no shopping ahead at all. But we are able here to get very fresh fish, which is something.
March 23rd: We went shopping and couldn't get anything. Butchers shut, fish shop shut, long queues outside the bakers, grocers half-empty . . . There is too much "under-the-counter" shopping here, too much put aside for special customers.
April 22nd: We had to have potatoes and cauliflower for dinner because there was no meat and the fish smelt—though plenty of people were queuing for it.
April 28th: I walked all round the town, but couldn't buy anything for dinner, so we fell back on fried eggs.

Milk and tea were sometimes difficult. In May William Stock in Chelmsford noted:

> My landlady finds that making the tea ration go round is one of her biggest problems. "I have never seen my cupboard so bare," she says.[6]

Queuing was a way of life, and occasionally the queues were of such proportions that the police took a hand. Their action was questioned at a meeting of Ipswich Council in May, when the chairman of the Watch Committee said queues had sometimes had to be broken up to prevent obstruction of the highway. He added that his committee had come to no conclusion as to whether queuing was the best method of ensuring distribution of foodstuffs in short supply.

Children had their rations supplemented by school meals. A government paper published in May, 1943, showed that nearly half of secondary-school children were getting school meals, and over a fifth of children in elementary schools. Educational authorities in most of East Anglia improved on these figures:

	Elementary schools	Secondary schools
East Suffolk	40%	55%
West Suffolk	19%	52%
Norfolk	19%	—
Cambridgeshire	29%	55%
Essex	24%	60%
Isle of Ely	9%	31%

Opposite page:
Experienced farmworkers
were called upon to teach
young people who
volunteered to help on the
farms. At Whissonsett in
Norfolk the local
agricultural club provided
classes at which youngsters
were taught how to hoe.
Lowestoft Journal

Right: Young people were
also encouraged to join
youth organisations such
as the St John cadets,
here seen on parade in
Cambridge. *Cambridge
Local Collection*

West Suffolk reported that it was serving 420,000 meals a year, compared with 100,000 at the outbreak of war. School canteens were "an unqualified success", children's health had improved and there was less absenteeism. Milk was supplied to well over half the pupils in schools of all kinds in every part of the region, and in some schools to over eighty per cent. The government requested that meals should be provided for at least three in four schoolchildren, and the eastern counties quickly responded and improved their provision later in the year.

Health did not suffer seriously as a result of food shortages. A distinguished physician, Lord Horder, declared that the nation was fit because of two important changes in habit: most people were eating more wholemeal bread and many more people were drinking pasteurised milk. The annual report of the Ipswich Schools Medical Officer of Health in June found that thirty-four per cent of schoolchildren there were graded "excellent" in nutritional tests, compared with only twenty-one per cent a year earlier.

A fifty-year-old East Bergholt woman offered this testimony:

> I am a stone lighter, but very well. I think the smaller protein content of the food has been very good for me . . . Most of the people that I meet are thinner than they were but, on the whole, in good health and demanding less of life, and therefore more satisfied. Only those people who are living in a state of constant anxiety for some loved person on active service seem to have had their health affected. I have had several very tired war workers here for recuperation, but they recover very quickly after a good rest and plenty of good country fare, which can still be got if you work for it.[7]

117

What was lacking in supplies was compensated for by a constant flow of advice. The Ministry of Food Centre in Cambridge sent a caravan around Norfolk and Suffolk villages during the summer months distributing recipes and giving demonstrations in village halls or around the caravan on any suitable open space. Housewives were shown how to make meals with a minimum of meat and a maximum of home-grown produce, how to bottle fruit, and how to make the best use of new products like dried eggs.

There was one "remarkable new food powder" that they were denied, although Lord Woolton, the Minister, had drawn attention to it during a visit to East Anglian food factories in May. This was mashed potato powder, which, his lordship averred, "only requires the addition of hot water to produce mashed potato identical with that prepared in the normal way". A Ministry Press handout said it was all going to the Forces:

> Housewives and bachelors will learn with regret that they will still have to carry on peeling potatoes, since the powder will not be available to the public for a very long time, all supplies having been earmarked for the government.

Food supplies remained difficult throughout 1943. When Christmas came the Ministry of Food decreed that puddings sold in shops should not exceed two pounds in weight. It produced what it termed "a reasonable supply" of biscuits, and a shipment of oranges arrived in time for one to appear in the stockings of most children in East Anglia.

Clothes rationing was also continued throughout the year, with much ingenuity shown in the efforts to ease its impact. The Women's Voluntary Service established a "Shoe Exchange" in the larger towns, where:

> Mothers are invited to bring in outgrown shoes in good condition and exchange them for a larger second-hand pair. No money or coupons will pass.

There had been considerable difficulty in getting small sizes in shoes, and the scheme was so successful that in Cambridge and Norwich it was soon supplemented by children's clothing exchanges.

Clothes rationing led an increasing number of women to wear trousers, in the face of strong male prejudice. Women staff employed by the Saffron Walden Borough Council asked the bachelor Mayor for permission to wear slacks in the office, saying they were short of coupons, could not buy stockings and were cold. He referred the matter to a meeting of the full council, at which there was opposition—one councillor thought slacks undesirable for those who had to deal with the public but acceptable for typists! In December, permission was granted.

Shortages of material and labour also forced a major sartorial change in Cambridge. The university issued an official decree on 28th April that until further notice undergraduates were excused from wearing, or carrying, "squares"—more familiarly known as mortarboards—which had been obligatory on all formal occasions and at all times when undergraduates went out after dark.

From 1st January, 1943, a trickle of utility furniture came into the shops. The introduction of such "utility" goods, replacing normal production lines in factories, enabled savings to be made in labour and materials. Maximum retail prices were fixed; "utility" goods were free of purchase tax, and they were often restricted to special classes of customer—in the case of furniture to newlyweds and the bombed-out. An advertisement for Dennes, of Norwich, promised: *"You can furnish three rooms with this excellent quality utility furniture for £70."*

Coal rationing was strict, but was eased as the winter ended—for the three months April to June householders in the eastern region were permitted one ton. Fortunately, it was the mildest winter for thirty years, with temperatures in January and February averaging 46.5 degrees. During the middle week of April the mean daily maximum temperature in Ipswich reached 68.6 degrees, and May had the highest sunshine figure since 1922.

The government was intent upon mobilising and conserving every material resource. There were two ways of doing this: by salvaging useful materials for reprocessing and by strict control of the way in which materials were used in the factories.

During the summer the Ministry of Works began a scrap metal drive in the Eastern Region. What was described as a "mobile sweep team of women locators" was sent first into Norfolk and later into East Suffolk, and it was announced that

The Royal Navy took part in the opening of the Wings for Victory Week at Norwich. Crowds turned out to watch the parade, which was a mile in length. *Lowestoft Journal*

"every village in the area will be searched for scrap metal". Headquarters were established first at Norwich and later at Saxmundham.

In some areas complaints were heard about the way that metal was seized; one farmer declared that two of his farm machines had been taken while his back was turned. At South Cambridgeshire RDC meeting in March the chairman declared that in one village all the cottages had lost their handgates but the railings around the "big house" park remained. The clerk explained that the Ministry of Works decided who was sent requisition notices, and a member remarked, in tones of biblical finality: "Some are left and some are taken, and it is no use saying anything or doing anything about it."

Norfolk and Suffolk organised a drive between 26th June and 10th July to collect books, paper, metal, rags, bones and rubber. Two million books were sought, but the organisers were careful to explain that they would not be pulped—they were to be used for the Forces, blitzed libraries and munitions.

Paper was not the only thing in short supply. Millers' music shop in Cambridge advertised in January:

GRAMOPHONE RECORDS WANTED
**Gramophone records must be returned to record dealers
if supplies are to be maintained.**
2½d paid for 10-inch, 4d for 12-inch.

Although most goods were in short supply, many who were still civilians were earning more money than ever before, mainly because of the overtime they were required to work. Labour claimed that "the £ is now worth only twelve shillings," but Mrs Williams met a woman in Sheringham whom she had once employed as her "charlady", and noted in her diary in September:

> She doesn't need to work now, Her daughter and son-in-law are both factory workers, earning between them £14 a week. She wasn't a bit pleased at the thought that the war would soon end.

In addition to rationing essentials, therefore, the government was intent on taking as much money as possible out of circulation in order to avoid inflation, and the budget of April, 1943, presented by Sir Kingsley Wood, clearly demonstrated this purpose.

The Chancellor did not raise income tax, but he put a penny on a pint of beer and 2s 4d on a bottle of whisky. Cigarettes which had cost a shilling for ten went up to 1s 2d. Purchase Tax, which had been levied at 66⅔ per cent, now went up to 100 per cent. The Chancellor declared that "there was an appreciable margin of personal expenditure on non-essentials which could and should be curtailed".

The war was costing £15 million a day, the Chancellor announced. Later in the year the Chancellor devised a Pay-as-you-earn tax plan, to come into operation in

April, 1944, which would enable the Treasury to collect its revenue more quickly. The Chancellor died suddenly on 21st September, the day before publication of his White Paper.

The big savings drive in 1943 took the form of a Wings for Victory campaign, with the emphasis of its propaganda on the RAF. It ran in every town and village during the early summer, and in the Eastern Region the total sum collected was £30,182,019, which was 20.7 per cent more than had been raised by the Warship Weeks in 1942. Virtually every town exceeded the target it had set itself, as these examples indicate:

	Target	*Amount collected*
Norwich	£1,000,000	£1,456,363
Cambridge	£750,000	£997,762
Ipswich	£700,000	£927,000
Colchester	£300,000	£469,212
Great Yarmouth	£280,000	£358,000
Saffron Walden	£200,000	£305,000
Lowestoft	£250,000	£280,000
Braintree	£150,000	£258,000
Bury St Edmunds	£180,000	£242,000
Huntingdon	£120,000	£135,763
Felixstowe	£70,000	£100,000
Newmarket	£80,000	£98,153
Saxmundham	£60,000	£92,500
Sudbury	£50,000	£86,000

The Norwich total of £1,456,363 represented £11 10s per head of the population; before this campaign, Norwich had saved £10,633,426 since the outbreak of war.

Mr Richard Stokes, the Labour MP for Ipswich, relentlessly continued his criticisms of the savings campaigns. When Ipswich announced its Wings for Victory savings week in May he publicly challenged the organiser:

> Can Mr (A.V.) Bishop truthfully tell the people of Ipswich that a single extra aeroplane will be provided, however much or little they subscribe? The important point is that spending must be restricted whilst goods are in short supply.

A spokesman for the savings movement replied:

> It is, of course, true that no fewer bombers or machine-guns would be made if War Savings certificates were relegated to the limbo of forgotten things . . . The mass of investors in war certificates do not, regrettably, have current accounts in the joint stock banks . . . Mr Stokes should look with benevolence on propaganda directed to two ends—to restrict senseless spending and to discourage the "stocking under the bed".

An unrepentant Mr Stokes fired back:

> I believe that the most patriotic action any citizen can take is to lend his money direct to the government free of interest. Unfortunately, this would be a precedent unpleasing to the banks . . .

He does not appear to have greatly influenced his constituents, for Ipswich exceeded its Wings for Victory target by nearly a third and proudly announced that it had raised a total of £9,099,000 in the various savings campaigns since the outbreak of war.

Apart from saving, the public was constantly urged to give to Red Cross, prisoners-of-war funds and other similar "good causes", and its response was always generous. In Suffolk an appeal for £50,000 for prisoners-of-war was launched on 1st July. There were many individual efforts, like that of Councillor Stanley Wilson, the first Labour Mayor of Saffron Walden, who paraded the streets of the town with a street organ playing *There'll always be an England*. Every organisation did its share of fund-raising activities, and fetes and other events were always well supported.

No matter how much the government asked of the people, it seemed, they could always find a little extra to offer on their own initiative.

An advertisement for the Freebridge Lynn Wings for Victory Week. *Lynn News and Advertiser*

CHAPTER EIGHT

Trying to Keep Cheerful

T HE STATE of public morale during 1943 did not remain steady or consistent. It was generally understood that the darkest days of the war had passed, but it was also recognised that a long, hard struggle lay ahead; this incongruity of experience and hope created ambivalence in the attitudes of most people. The Mass Observation organisation, which regularly collected information from its investigators all over the country about the state of public morale, reported in January, 1943, that:

> Cheerfulness remained at its high level of last month . . . With the continued success of the Russians, there was a growing optimism about the likely length of the war . . .[1]

Prime Minister Winston Churchill did his best to boost morale with a two-hour speech to Parliament on 11th February recounting successes in North Africa and closer co-operation with the Americans. "I thought I had a good tale to tell," he remarked afterwards, and the Press agreed, for the front page of the *Eastern Daily Press* was dominated by the headlines:

MOST BUOYANT SPEECH SINCE THE WAR

Premier's tonic for the Commons

But many of the public failed to respond. Mrs Sarah Williams noted in her diary soon afterwards:

> I am surprised to find that people are very little excited about the victories in Tunisia. I begin to see signs of war weariness.[2]

At about the same time William Stock, in Chelmsford, was recording a similar impression:

> Referring to a remark by a radio commentator last night that "there is no sign of war weariness", my landlady said: "Everyone I meet is war-weary, fed up to the hilt with it." The commentator probably meant that there has been no great lowering of spirits, but all the same the way the war drags on and on is becoming more and more monstrous.[3]

Rumour was rife. Mrs Williams offered an example on 17th March:

> Someone is going round telling people what to do if there should be German commando raids. M. S. says she was told that there had already been raids on this coast and some people had, in fact, been kidnapped.

Another clue to the climate of the times was given by Winifred Last in Bury St Edmunds, in a diary entry on 11th March:

> Nine-tenths of my time I do not say what I really think when in conversation with other people, and in these days, when anybody can be imprisoned for dropping a careless remark, I think most of us must say what it appears expedient to say, rather than what we think. It is the only safe thing to do.[4]

But such inhibitions were not widespread. During the summer Mrs Williams

> . . . went into the confectioners to find almost an indignation meeting because of Churchill going to America, and especially because Mrs Churchill and Mary went with him. It was the attitude of: "We're told not to have holidays, why should they?", "I bet they're not living on rationed foods", and "I expect Mrs Churchill needs some new clothes."

In May Mass Observation reported on the situation in Peterborough:

> Like most towns at the present time, Peterborough is in a state of social upheaval. Its old routine of life has been completely disorganised by the war. New industries, and expansion of old, have brought thousands of strangers to the town, and, as in all these cases, there is a good deal of friction between the new and old populations. Shopping, billets, jobs—all these become a source of grievance to one or other party . . .[5]

Many families in East Anglia were living on or near the poverty line. A deputation from the Family Endowment Society which saw the Chancellor of the Exchequer, Sir Kingsley Wood, in January urged him to introduce State family allowances in his Budget. For a family consisting of a man, wife and three children, paying thirteen shillings a week rent, the poverty line was £3 12s 7d a week, it argued. Even some of the nation's most acclaimed war heroes were not getting that much, as the Ipswich public was reminded during February. John Hannah, invalided out of the RAF, where he had been a flight sergeant and had been the youngest man to win the Victoria Cross, Britain's highest award for conspicuous bravery in the presence of the enemy, appeared as a one-man act on the stage at the Ipswich Hippodrome. Relating the story of how he had beaten out a fire in a bomber hit in a raid, he excused himself: "The only reason I am doing this is for the money it will bring me." He explained that he had a wife and a child and his pension was only only £3 11s 3d a week.

Winifred Last met a young woman pushing a pram around Bury St Edmunds during June and noted:

> She said she had never been so hungry anywhere as in Bury. She was supposed to share a kitchen with the other people in the house, but did not, as it was awkward waiting for saucepans and so on, and everybody having to fit in with everybody else's cooking. She said sometimes she took home fish and chips and the fish and chip shops were a Godsend. It would be interesting to know how many bombed-out women and soldiers' wives spend their days pushing prams around the country.

Overcrowding in temporary accommodation compounded the problems, particularly in Cambridge, where the population had increased from 50,000 to 80,000 during the first four years of war. The Mayoress and the wife of the Regional Commissioner declared in a statement in January that there were "instances of women sleeping in air raid shelters and bus shelters". Backed by every leading women's organisation in the town, they raised money to take over Benet House, in Brooklands Avenue, as a hostel for eighteen of the civilian women drafted into Cambridge to work.

The Town Clerk told the March meeting of Cambridge Town Council that he had looked into twenty-one complaints of extortionate rents being charged for accommodation, furnished and unfurnished, and found fifteen cases proved.

Winifred Last listed poor housing among her tribulations in Bury:

> Oh, to be back in Bexhill in 1939, on my beam ends for money, but able to buy a cake and bananas and cream! Gone are those days, I fear, beyond recall. I had a gas ring there, too, and electric light, and a sink and a water tap, and a nice landlord, and friends and laughter, and the sea and sunshine. I was thinking today that when the war is over I shall look back on Bury St Edmunds and think how I have wasted these war years by not being happy here. Life here has been bearable. It has been fairly pleasant, and on the whole people have been pretty decent, Nevertheless, I do not "live" but only exist. I never really laugh in Bury St Edmunds or relax.

Poor housing conditions and inadequate incomes had been features of pre-war life in East Anglia, so that the hardships which now caused people to complain were not entirely attributable to the war. Complaints heard at the annual meeting of the West Suffolk Federation of Women's Institutes at Bury St Edmunds in June had been voiced many times before. A lady from Borley said they had one pump on the village green and some of the cottages which it served were more than a mile away. At Cavendish, it was related, there was an urgent need for piped water and more stand-pipes. Delegates from many other villages complained that they had no telephone and no Post Office within two miles.

Some mothers who had to endure bad housing conditions simply walked out of them. The Cambridge and District branch of the NSPCC, in its annual report, said: "The war years have shown a considerable increase in the number of children left alone at night. There have been several cases of young mothers, whose husbands are serving in the Forces, leaving their homes at night for social entertainment, not realising the danger to which they are exposing their children."

Parental control of children—which was now usually the responsibility of a mother alone—became more difficult. Mrs Sarah Williams' experience in March was typical:

> There are empty houses on either side of us and we spend our time chasing children out of them. They steal anything available, and do any damage possible. Mr A———, to whom one belongs, says "What is to happen to these children after the war? There is no discipline; they are just dragged up."

The number of young delinquents increased everywhere. Two boys, aged nine and ten, who were found guilty in January of wilful damage to St Andrew's Church at Cherry Hinton, near Cambridge, used a pickaxe to hack at one of the pillars and wrought havoc among the furnishings. "The church had been wrecked," said a witness. In July four boys, aged twelve to fifteen, were charged, also at Cambridge, with breaking and entering a Home Guard headquarters and taking twelve sticks of gelignite. They had made two attempts to light them, once in a house and once on a railway line. Two of the boys asked for a series of other offences to be taken into consideration, involving 250 rounds of ammunition and sixteen hand grenades. One of the grenades was found down a drain at Pembroke College and a bomb disposal man had to be engaged to deal with it. The boys were bound over for two years. An eighteen-year-old youth who was sent to prison for a year for looting from bombed shops in Great Yarmouth was told by the magistrates' clerk: "If the case had gone to the Assizes you could have been hanged." The usual run of juvenile cases, however, concerned theft, with occasional cases of embezzlement and arson.

All the county authorities gave much attention to their young people. Essex Education Committee organised local conferences in Chelmsford, Colchester, Walthamstow and Dagenham, and received a summary of their findings at a meeting on 25th January. The committee was told that:

> Strong comments were made at each conference on the lack of parental control and responsibility. The question of religious training was also to the fore, and the decline in home training and Sunday Schools was advanced as another factor.

The report added that the conferences had revealed "the usual divergence of views on the subject of corporal punishment", and had left a "general impression" that corporal punishment was still necessary in certain instances. The Education Committee was able to take into account, however, a statement from the Chief Constable of Essex that there had been a recent falling off in juvenile crime, which he attributed to the committee's policy of opening youth centres. (He added that there had been a distinct rise in crime by eighteen- to twenty-two-year-olds, due, he suggested, to their desire to get out of the Army.) The committee's decisions, after weighing all the evidence, were to establish a child guidance clinic, with a trained psychiatrist in charge; to make greater efforts to improve attendance at schools and to give more careful attention to the standard of religious education; to publish a pamphlet on the training of children, and to plan for post-war courses for parents; to propose that cinemas should not open during the hours when Sunday Schools were in session; and to recommend the Home Office to appoint younger Justices of the Peace, with greater representation of parents, particularly working-class parents.

In West Suffolk the problems seemed less acute, and its Education Committee was informed in April that absenteeism from school was down and that "training in manners and behaviour has been very effective", which it attributed in part to the

Lord Somers, Lord Baden-Powell's successor as Chief Scout, visited Ipswich in May. In spite of the date at the head of the page this was 1943.
East Anglian Daily Times

EAST ANGLIAN DAILY TIMES, TUESDAY, MAY 25, 1934

IPSWICH: The Chief Scout of the British Empire (Lord Somers) was the guest of honour at an Ipswich L.A. camp fire at the Northgate School for Boys playing field on Saturday evening. In the front row of the group are (left to right): Scouter C. T. Dawson, the Deputy Chief Scout (Sir Percy Everett), Canon C. O. George (Ipswich District Commissioner), Lord Somers, Scouter A. W. Hurrel (Imperial H.Q. Secretary), A. C. C. Norman Allen (Hon. Secretary, Suffolk Boy Scouts Association), Miss Gibb (Assistant Divisional Guide Commissioner), and Miss King (County Akela Leader). (Inset) Sir Percy Everett and Lord Somers. (E.A.D.T. photos.)

introduction of school meals. "From the social side, it has proved of great advantage to the life of the school."

The Scout movement prospered. The annual meeting of the Suffolk Scout Council was told in May that membership in the county had increased from 1,503 to 2,514 in two years. Bury had increased its strength from 113 to 480, and Stowmarket had 113 Scouts, whereas in 1941 the organisation in that area had been "in abeyance". When the Chief Scout, Lord Somers, toured the county in that same month there were impressive rallies at Bury St Edmunds, Haverhill and Ipswich. In July the Chief Guide, Lady Baden-Powell, visited Suffolk. At Ipswich a thousand Guides and three hundred Brownies attended a camp fire on the Alderman Road recreation ground, and later there were rallies at Halesworth, Wickham Market and Little Waldingfield, and a Guide service in Bury Cathedral. Lady Baden-Powell's message was that "the world is crying out for kindness and goodwill. We as Guides can make the world a happier place in the days to come."

What brought adult offenders before the courts? There were frequent cases of burglary and house-breaking, particularly in Cambridge and some of the coastal areas, but the majority of offenders were not in that league. A procession of motorists were prosecuted for exceeding the 20 mph speed limit that applied during blackout hours. Their usual excuse was that they were concentrating so hard on seeing where they were going that they could not glance at the speedometer. Large numbers of cyclists were fined for not having lights; *their* usual excuse was that they could not get batteries. The Mayor of Lowestoft found himself facing his own bench of magistrates in May, accused of showing a light during blackout hours at his residence at Oulton Broad. *His* excuse was that "there is evidently a fault somewhere, caused by the weather", and he pleaded not guilty; but the bench reminded him of what he had said to other offenders, and fined him £1. Theft of bicycles was another frequent offence, and there were some prosecutions for wasting food, as when a sixty-year-old woman was fined £40 at Hunts Quarter Sessions for feeding loaves to her horses.

Very few cases of drunkenness were brought to court. At the brewster sessions in most of the main towns the police reported remarkable sobriety.

Most towns and villages maintained a full round of entertainment, but there were novel variations on the usual fare, with a strong American flavour to much of the social activity. The Rex Cinema in Cambridge had to turn away many who could not be packed in for a January show "presented by a group of Uncle Sam's boys"—hill-billy songs, Hawaian guitars and square dancing. There were "Welcome America Balls" at Cambridge Guildhall in February and April and a

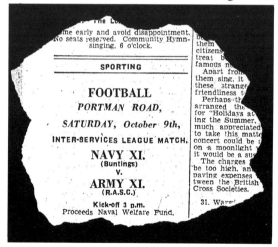

Services football teams took part in contests that helped to provide popular entertainment.   *Lowestoft Journal*

first "At Home" at the Guildhall in August for fifty American officers. In November the *Cambridge Daily News* reported:

> The Corn Exchange has housed many functions in its time, but one never so unusual and picturesque as the Barn Dance staged there last night by the American Red Cross for US forces in the district. The occasion was the celebration of the traditional American custom, Hallowe'en . . . Halfway through the dance a cabaret programme (or "floor show", as our visitors have it) was put on by members of an American Red Cross entertainment unit . . . The famous American Flying Eagles band kept up a continuous programme of really "hot" music. Around the sides of the hall were crates of apples and pears from which the many dancers, numbering about 1,800, were at liberty to help themselves . . .

An Anglo-American Services party at Cambridge Guildhall on Christmas Eve, with a hundred and fifty US officers and men and a similar number of girls from the

British women's services, was featured in a special coast-to-coast broadcast in the USA, with Gilbert Harding as one of the compères.

Everywhere the cinema and dancing remained the most popular forms of entertainment, but they did not always offer escapism. The majority of feature films (and almost everything in the newsreels which were an essential part of every programme) had a fighting flavour. Popular films included Noel Coward's "In Which We Serve", "Desert Victory", "Coastal Command" and "Flying Fortress". And at any dance-hall where Americans regularly attended an enquiry of "Where's Tex (or Hank, or Jim)?" might be answered with a shake of the head, or "He didn't make it back".

Theatres were always full in the larger towns, and amateur organisations continued to present concert performances. Some of the commercial theatres had difficulty finding talent enough to fill their needs. An advertisement in the 8th May issue of the *Lowestoft Journal and Mercury* read:

VARIETY ATTRACTIONS WANTED!

Bands, Pianists, Vocalists, Dancers, Acrobats, etc.

Also Good Juveniles and Girls for Dancing Troupes.

Good Amateurs and **Members of the Forces** 'specially welcome for our new Stage Shows.

Apply now for audition to Manager

EMPIRE CINEMA
GT. YARMOUTH
'Phone 3147

Classical music attracted large audiences whenever it was available, which was very frequently in Cambridge, fairly often in Norwich, and occasionally in Ipswich, Colchester and Chelmsford. Cambridge attracted all the leading performers, as for example on a Sunday evening in April when an Arts Theatre audience heard Benjamin Britten and Clifford Curzon at two pianos, with tenor Peter Pears, performing for the first time in Britain two works which Britten had just composed.

The cultural life of Norwich was given a boost when in October Mr Russell Colman informed the City Council that he proposed to bequeath to the city his collection of pictures and drawings of the Norwich School "in token of my affection for the city of my birth, and in acknowledgement of the honour and the unfailing courtesy and kindness I have received from my fellow citizens." The bequest was to include sufficient funds for a suitable gallery. There were more than forty pictures by John Crome, the founder of the School, and thirty-one oil paintings and five hundred water-colours, monochromes and drawings in chalk or pencil by John Sell Cotman. Paul Oppé, a former deputy director of the Victoria and Albert Museum, called it "the greatest benefaction of British painting since Turner bequeathed the contents of his gallery to the nation."

There was not much sport, although local matches with scratch teams, usually drawn from the Services, were arranged most weekends in the big towns. In August Ipswich Town Football Club, with its eye on the future, signed seventeen-year-old Denis Edward Shurman, of Devizes, a centre-forward who had scored 108 goals for Devizes Rangers during the previous season. It was the club's first signing since the outbreak of war.

The Americans offered something new: baseball. It took English spectators some while to understand what was going on; when the Kentucky Rebels played the Yankee Eagles on Fenners Ground at Cambridge the reporter for the local newspaper obviously lacked the appropriate vocabulary:

> The players brought with them full equipment for the occasion and the catcher and one of the umpires were clothed in that padded rigout which some may have seen on the screen. They looked like medieval knights. Then there was the batter. In the customary fashion, he wielded his cudgel-like instrument and attempted to send the ball for six—if we may use the English phraseology. The fielders had a glove-shaped leather affair on one hand, so as to enable them to catch the ball more effectively.

Racing continued at Newmarket, although not without interruption. On 12th May an RAF plane crashed on the course and caused so much damage that it took several days to clear up; the occupants of the plane died. The 2,000 Guineas and the 1,000 Guineas were postponed for a week. The Derby was run on 19th June and won by Miss Dorothy Paget's Straight Deal. Two thousand people cycled to the course, and the evening before the race stranded visitors offered inhabitants £2 to sit for a few hours in an armchair; scores of them spent the night in the open. What in peacetime was the big event of Royal Ascot, The Gold Cup, was run at Newmarket on 7th July and was won by eight lengths by Gordon Richards on an outsider, Ujiji, in what the local newspaper described as "a race devoid of the slightest degree of excitement". It drew more visitors from London than had the Derby.

The weather had its effect upon morale, and the exceptionally good weather during the early months of the year cheered flagging spirits. At mid-February the Chelmsford diarist, William Stock, noted:

I think we have had more sunshine this winter than last summer. Today was almost like a day in June. It makes you feel good to be alive, war or no war.

In Cambridge another diarist, John Creevey, greeted March thus:

I have noticed that many people have bought Spring flowers this week—there is a flower stall every day in the Market Place. Some of the suburban housewives seem to be busy doing the Spring cleaning.

A great gale swept Britain on Tuesday, 6th April, and North Norfolk caught its full fury, with 80 mph winds and big seas. At Cley water streamed up the village main street and entered the telephone exchange, causing a temporary interruption of service, and at Beccles a 50-foot hose-drying tower was uprooted and fell on a first-aid post. Many roads in Suffolk were blocked by fallen trees and earth was whirled up from fields. But the good weather quickly returned, and William Stock noted twelve days later that in Chelmsford:

. . . the weather is a dominant topic at the moment. I don't think anyone remembers such hot weather in April. The gardens need rain, though.

A few weeks later the Nature Notes in the *Lowestoft Journal* were lyrical:

In this especially enchanted May [we] find the whole of the English countryside nothing else but one great flower garden spread before enraptured eyes.

There was more unseasonably fine weather later in the year, but by then it had ceased to have a tonic effect. Mrs Williams noted at the end of October that Sheringham folk "complain it's unseasonable", and when it gave way a week later to lower temperatures, they still grumbled:

It's a bitterly cold day. People are complaining all over the place about their clothes. They are getting thin and no coupons to replace them. Everything everywhere is getting shoddier and shoddier.

The exceptional amount of sunshine during the summer, however, enabled everyone to make the best of another year of "holidays at home". Every town organised its own programme of summer entertainment. Colchester, for example, arranged a seven-week programme of special events, most of them staged in Castle Park and the Recreation Grounds. An advance announcement read:

Teas will be served in the Lower Castle Park. As you are all aware, it is found impossible to provide crockery, therefore it must be clearly understood that tea can only be supplied to those bringing their own cups—the ORGANISERS HAVE NONE AVAILABLE. Failure to comply with this request will result in refusal, for which we offer no apology.

In Ipswich on 1st August the Mayor opened a "Stay-at-Home Holiday Week", the Band of the Oxfordshire and Buckinghamshire Light Infantry played in Christchurch Park, and those who turned up were informed that "the WVS have arranged for the sale of tea in customers' own cups". In Cambridge 7,250 paid for admission to the town football ground for an August Bank Holiday programme of sporting events and music by the pipers of the Seaforth Highlanders, and on the same day there were over 7,000 on the Wellesley Recreation Ground at Great Yarmouth for a sports meeting and Fire Service display.

Apart from these programmes, there seemed no limit to the enthusiasm for pageantry and parades, and the savings campaign provided plenty of opportunities. On a Sunday afternoon during March British and American services, local Civil Defence services and various youth organisations took part in one of the most imposing parades ever seen in Bury St Edmunds, to inaugurate Wings for Victory week; thousands of people lined the streets, and the services in the cathedral and St Mary's were packed. In May the two Norwich battalions of the Home Guard staged a march-past in front of the City Hall and a demonstration—"every man in full battle equipment". In September the Old Contemptibles held their annual parade at Great St Mary's in Cambridge, marching from Parker's Piece and around Market Hill, with the band of the US Engineers at their head, and a week later there was a

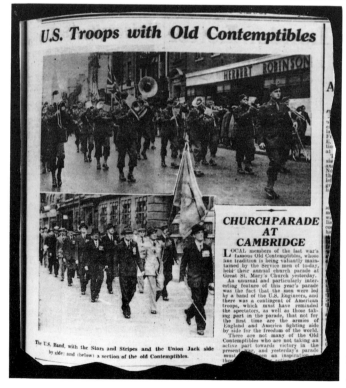

At Cambridge the Old Contemptibles, veterans of the 1914 BEF, were led to church by the band of an American engineer battalion. *Cambridge Local Collection*

"Grand Victory March" of units of the United States, British and Polish forces, with the flags of all nations paraded from Parker's Piece around the town. September 25th was "Battle of Britain Sunday", with another church parade at Great St Mary's and another procession from Parker's Piece, with all the Services represented and the Home Guard band at the head.

When the government devised new themes for demonstrations—one was for "Farm Sunday"—one clergyman, the Rev. A. Morris, Vicar of St Mary's at Huntingdon, wrote in his parish magazine: "I believe we are all getting heartily sick of the special Sundays." He declared that many of those who produced these "novel ideas" and seemed so keen to observe them ignored the traditional Christian festivals.

But members of the Royal Family made frequent appearances at these parades—the Princess Royal, the Duchess of Kent and the Duchess of Gloucester all visited Cambridge—and that always brought out big crowds.

Honours were disbursed in recognition of distinguished service, decorations to those in the Services, orders and awards to encourage "the great and the good" in civilian life. In the New Year's Honours List knighthoods were bestowed on Professor John Harold Clapham, Vice Provost of King's College, Cambridge, and President of the British Academy, and the Clerk to East Suffolk County Council, Mr Cecil Oakes. The Town Clerk of Great Yarmouth, Mr Farra Conway, received an OBE for his services to Civil Defence; and MBEs were awarded to Mr William Henry Crates, Chief Air Raid Warden at Lowestoft; Miss Eveline Elsie Mansey, matron of Lowestoft and North Suffolk Hospital; Mrs Margaret Hitchcock, vice-chairman of the West Suffolk executive, National Federation of Women's Institutes; Mr Aubrey Thorn Chittock, Commander, Norwich City Special Constabulary; Mr Victor Ernest Harrison, Chief Air Raid Warden at Norwich; and Miss Doris Beatrice Lane, matron of the City Maternity Home in Norwich.

At a special meeting of Bury St Edmunds Town Council on 10th May the Freedom of the town was conferred on the Marquis of Bristol, who was in his eightieth year, "in recognition of his services to the borough". He had lived at Ickworth for forty-four years, had been Hereditary Steward of the Liberty of Bury, MP for the borough, twenty years chairman of West Suffolk County Council, and twenty-seven years president of West Suffolk Hospital. The Hervey family, it was recalled, had given the Shirehall to Bury and an earlier Marquis had contributed largely to the provision of the Corn Exchange. Lord Bristol said his family had been intimately associated with Bury for over five hundred years, since one of his forebears had married the heiress to Ickworth in 1457.

The biggest boost to morale, however, was probably the return home during the autumn of a number of men who had been held as prisoners-of-war in German camps. The idea of men returning from the war had a tonic effect and caused much local celebration. It was a foretaste of what, it was hoped, would be the common experience. Nine men returned to King's Lynn, six to Norwich, three to Cambridge and several more to other parts of the region. A Norwich airman, Sergeant Arthur Ronald Mason, who returned in October after two and a half years as a prisoner, after being shot down over Holland on a raid, brought news that at Stalag 8b camp there were two hundred or so prisoners from Norfolk, Suffolk and Cambridgeshire and they had formed an East Anglian POW Association, to protect their interests then and after the war.

There were some signs of a revival of interest in religion, as an entry in Mrs Sarah Williams' diary indicated:

> What a lot of books are being written now about the life of the spirit. There is a hunger for religion everywhere.

Her second child, an 8½-lb son, arrived on 10th June, and when he was christened she volunteered to become a Sunday School teacher in Sheringham. Her thoughts at this time seemed far removed from the wartime scene. She had become an enthusiastic gardener. One day she was busy removing the glass from the old picture frames to makes cloches and on other days she was reading books by Adrian Bell, A. G. Street and Henry Williamson—and seed catalogues. She reached a profound conclusion:

> Once I wanted a good job and social position for Jacob, but never very desperately. Now I prefer some land, some bees, a goat—and plenty of babies. There must be quite a movement of this sort.

If some women were affected spiritually by wartime conditions, many, many more were affected in contrary ways—and for them there were often more babies than they wanted.

Economist Lord Keynes was made High Steward of Cambridge at a ceremony on 6th March. He was pleased to speculate that he was probably the first in four centuries who had actually been born in the town. *Cambridge Local Collection*

CHAPTER NINE

"A heart-breaking thing . . ."

IT WAS generally understood that men in the Services, far from home, needed feminine company in their off-duty hours, but by the opening months of 1943 the government and many of the local authorities in East Anglia had become seriously concerned about social problems which had arisen in both towns and villages. Some of these problems arose from fraternisation of young girls and women with soldiers and airmen, and particularly, it seemed, with Americans, who had so much more money to spend. Some, who were still schoolgirls, appeared to be beyond parental control, and among the older women were wives of serving soldiers, some with children.

The problems went deeper than the over-friendliness of local women. An eighteen-year-old girl living in Great Ashfield, near Bury St Edmunds, afterwards recalled that American airmen, "having found that we were not easy meat, or there on the base just to hop into bed with them, began importing train-loads of tarts from London, all fares paid". They were dubbed "shack rats"[1].

It was exceptional for any of them to be taken before a court, as were two girls from Leicester, aged eighteen and twenty, who pitched a tent inside the airbase near Eye, in Suffolk. A police inspector found them outside the tent with a black soldier, and inside there was a bed and some blankets. He told the magistrates at a March hearing: "The girls said they were asked by the boys to come down and there would be a room for them on arrival." The elder girl had three previous convictions. Both were sent to three months' hard labour for trespassing on Service land.

If there was little published evidence of straightforward prostitution, there was no doubt that illegitimate births and venereal disease were both increasing. Figures for illegitimate births were not published at the time, but they were certainly on a rising curve (see table on next page). Special problems arose if the children had black American fathers*.

At the annual meeting of the Ely Diocesan Association for Moral Welfare Work, the Assistant Bishop of Ely, the Rev. G.S. Walsh, observed that war

---

* It has never been established how many children had black American fathers. After the war newspapers and magazines estimated from 550 to 5,000. An investigation by Sylvia McNeill on behalf of the League of Coloured Peoples in 1945, when she collected information from county welfare officers, showed 553 brown babies born to 545 mothers, of whom 92 were married and 98 unmarried, with the marital status of the others unknown. Her figures showed six counties ahead of Suffolk: Devon, 83; Lancashire, 70; Gloucestershire, 60; Hampshire, 50; Somerset, 39; Cornwall, 38; Suffolk, 34. A later estimate was 700 to 1,000 babies. There were certainly more white than black American fathers.

conditions had put the whole country into a state of upheaval. He told his audience that the problems they had to deal with were world-wide and were also to be found in every village and parish throughout the country. The annual report to the meeting stated that twenty-four girls had been admitted to the maternity home during the year and twenty-one babies had been born, of whom three had died.

ILLEGITIMACY AND VENEREAL DISEASE[2]

	1939	1943	1944	1945
Cambridgeshire				
Illegitimate births	3.8%	202 = 7.8%	294 = 9.9%	348 = 13%
in Cambridge	4.3%	120 = 8.8%	178 = 11.6%	190 = 14.2%
in rural areas	3.3%	82 = 6.8%	116 = 8.1%	158 = 11.8%
VD first-time patients	209	493	461	369
males	131	276	230	183
females	78	217	231	186
VD under treatment				
during the year	365	639	—	519
males	212	372	—	268
females	153	267	—	251
West Suffolk				
Illegitimate births	60 = 4%	—	208 = 11%	296 = 18%
VD first-time patients	43	156	102	199
VD under treatment				
during the year	46	196	168	260
City and County of Norwich				
Illegitimate births	78 = 4.8%	192 = 11%	297 = 14%	414 = 19%
VD first-time patients	—	351	—	218
males		162		90
females		189		128
VD under treatment during				
the year (attendances)	—	777	—	966
males	—	393	—	363
females	—	384	—	603

As the New Year began, the number of cases of VD in the United Kingdom had risen seventy per cent since the outbreak of war and the Ministry of Health launched a big advertising campaign warning about the dangers and giving information about centres where advice and treatment were available. In May it was disclosed that VD had already put more than two thousand American GIs in Britain out of action so far that year, and the rate of infection was fifty per cent higher than among American troops in the USA[3]. East Anglia, simply because it had so many servicemen at large, had more than its fair share of this problem.

The *Eastern Daily Press* published an editorial on 19th February:

Today sees the beginning of an official publicity campaign by the Ministry of Health on the subject of venereal disease. The appearance of such frank advertisements on a subject which, by tacit consent, has hitherto for obvious reasons been practically taboo in the news columns of the lay Press is a departure from custom which will doubtless startle numbers of our readers. But the compelling facts of a recent large increase in the incidence of these diseases are, in our view, ample justification for any and every effort that the public health authorities can make to try to stamp them out.

The government had introduced in November, 1942, a regulation requiring any woman identified as a source of infection to be compulsorily treated. West Suffolk had seconded one of its county health visitors for special duties to implement this regulation, and during 1943 fifteen different women were reported and investigated. In Norwich forty-one women were similarly referred[4]. It was often difficult to implement the regulation because women were identified by their Christian names or nicknames only and without addresses.

Despite the government advertising, most people kept their eyes averted. Mrs Williams, the Sheringham diarist, noted:

My aunt came down and after a mention of VD said she hadn't any idea of what it was like. My mother confesses that neither has she and when I say "what dreadful ignorance" says: "You must remember that up 'til a few years ago we would have died rather than mention it".[5]

William Stock, in Chelmsford, confirmed that:

Mention of it in public is still not done in polite society.[6]

About the wider problems, however, there could be no pretence. Indeed it became a staple of conversation and gossip. A diarist in Bury St Edmunds, Miss Winifred Last, described a conversation in her office in March:

Tommy was saying I would not believe what this town is like at night. Air raid shelters are used for sexual purposes and made filthy . . . I hear that one of the maids in the annexe of Everards Hotel has been sharing her bed with a soldier or soldiers and that the case is coming up in court . . .[7]

Teenage boys and girls followed the Americans. With the boys, it was usually a case of "Gi' us some chewing gum, mister", but it was a different matter with the girls. A regular stream of cases before the courts revealed the situation: young women seeking paternity orders, young women accused of concealing the birth of babies, or abandoning infants, and one case, in June, of a twenty-year-old Ely girl charged with murder of her four-month-old son. In August a woman was sentenced to six months' imprisonment for keeping a brothel in Portugal Place, Cambridge, and at Norfolk Assizes in October two mothers were sent to prison for allowing servicemen to have carnal knowledge of their daughters, aged fifteen and fourteen, in their own homes. Abortionists appeared before courts in several towns, including Newmarket and Cambridge. In December two Ipswich girls, aged eighteen and nineteen, were placed on probation for two years for aiding and abetting a woman who was already in prison for keeping a brothel in North Hill, Colchester. They were sent to Salvation Army homes, but they both absconded, so they were brought back to court and imprisoned for three months.

Some young mothers were charged with neglect of their children, usually by leaving them unattended while they went to public houses or cinemas. Some children were brought before the courts because they were out of control of their parent(s).

The wording of some of the charges against women was strange. At Stowmarket, a twenty-four-year-old woman was fined £1 for "damaging growing crops by trespassing", after a constable had caught her lying in a field with a soldier, despite the fact that the farmer had put up barbed wire to keep out courting couples. She had left a pram nearby containing a year-old baby. Another young married woman was fined £1 by Dereham magistrates for "assuming a name other than that by which she was ordinarily known" after she had taken rooms in a farmhouse at Swanton Morley using the name of her RAF boyfriend.

Marriages were under strain. At the assizes at Norwich in June and October sixty-six decrees *nisi* were granted, and, after hearing these and other cases, Mr Justice Oliver observed: "Bigamy is today absolutely rife in this country . . . In every town one goes to there is bigamy after bigamy, and people seem to think it does not matter."

Not surprisingly, then, "moral welfare" was a subject of constant discussion in church, social, legal and local government circles, but the discussion was usually conducted in coded language. The words "prostitution", "immorality" and "venereal disease" passed few lips. Some public figures sought to camouflage the

A newspaper advertisement warning of the dangers of venereal disease. *East Anglian Daily Times*

whole problem, some became over-excited about it, while others tried hard to keep it in perspective.

The Bishop of Norwich, speaking in Lowestoft in June, offered a balanced view: he would not say that England had gone morally to the dogs or that the character of the younger generation was worse than ever before. "It is very easy to get hold of exaggerated ideas", he declared, "for there are far more good homes than ever, and far more young people standing firm amongst difficult conditions." But he admitted that the Home Office was seriously alarmed at the increase of venereal disease, and he said it would be criminal to shut their eyes to the need for moral welfare work. By October he was taking a more pessimistic view, in a pastoral letter read in all parish churches:

> We know that all is not well with the life of our nation . . . Nothing is more alarming than the decay of personal standards of sexual morality . . . The behaviour of many of our women—and peculiarly of quite young girls—in town and village alike in casual acquaintance with soldiers, English or foreign, is a disgrace to their sex and the nation . . .

The Bishop's remedy? "A much stronger public opinion, based on Christian conviction". The Bishop of Chelmsford struck a similar note in November:

> We have in Britain the loveliest girls, the neatest and prettiest girls that God ever made. That these girls are being marred and spoiled and destroyed in body and soul is a heart-breaking thing. I sometimes say I think the Christian religion is dying out. It is hanging by a thread in this country today. Faith has been abandoned by the vast majority of the people . . .

Other churchmen did not mince words. The Rev. A. Shillito, writing from Blofield Rectory in July, declared:

> It makes one's blood boil to see men of mature age behaving disgracefully with young girls who are but children. They are guilty of the worst form of sabotage, in destroying some of the most precious things we have, the womanhood and family life of England. Women are punished for soliciting, but what about the men? Fornication is not only a sin, but a crime against the community, and should be dealt with as such.

In November the Rev. Gilbert Laws wrote in the *Eastern Daily Press*:

> The position is rapidly becoming worse in the streets, and only those who have to be out and about at the closing time of places of amusement and public houses have any idea of the slump in public behaviour . . . Girls and young married women have complained to their ministers of being accosted, molested and "mauled about" by men when leaving religious meetings, clubs and classes held in the evening.

A Mass Observation Peterborough survey concluded:

> It simply isn't fit for a decent girl to walk through the streets at night now. There were, in fact, very few women in the streets at all in the evening.[8]

There were stories of nurses' homes, land girls' hostels and similar places literally besieged by GIs. The Mayor of Bury St Edmunds, Major E. L. D. Lake, said during the summer that he viewed with a great deal of apprehension the state of affairs in his town, where he thought the conditions were deplorable as a result of the war. Mass Observation sent one of its special investigators to Bury, and the resultant report gave a grim picture of conditions. It read, in part:

> The main result of the war has been to flood the town with American soldiers. There are a few service clubs and canteens, but in general the soldiers appear to have a boring time in the town, with little else to do in their spare time but to go to the pictures or flirt with the local girls.
>
> Of this latter activity a local cafe-keeper said: "There's a lot of immorality goes on in the town. I've seen some sights in this cafe. Early in the morning I've had young girls, fourteen to seventeen years old, waiting outside my doors with Americans for me to open so they can come in for some breakfast. You could see they'd been out all night by the bits of straw and hay all over them. My daughter has seen so much sin here that she has been made repugnant to it."
>
> Her daughter, a pretty girl of eighteen, joined in: "That's right. But what else is there to do but go for walks in the country? There are three cinemas here, and they're always full. If you can go to a dance, it's too crowded and full of Americans. There aren't any nice clubs to go to. There are only the pubs and country walks."[9]

The Ipswich Probation Officer, Miss Grant, told the East Suffolk Probation Committee that there was a special problem with young girls between thirteen and sixteen who attended dances and were found in public houses at half-time with their partners. She did not wish to kill dancing for young girls, she said, but some of the conduct was "appalling".

Mrs Williams noted in her diary:

> *September 24th:* Conditions in Norwich seem appalling. Mrs W——, head of the Girls' Secondary School, had to send for a doctor to address the senior girls on the subject of their relationship with American soldiers.

At the annual meeting of parents of the Blyth Secondary School at the Theatre Royal in Norwich in December, the headmistress reported that a series of talks had been given by a doctor to the girls in the middle and upper school on matters of hygiene and sex, because the dangers called for plain speaking. But she added that there had been "a spate of lies" about the girls and it had been asserted that large numbers had been expelled on moral grounds. There had not been one such case, she said, adding:

> I have nothing but contempt for the combination of credulity, spite and salacious enjoyment of filth which can make the citizens of Norwich besmirch the characters of defenceless girls.

The Medical Officer for Norwich, Dr V. F. Soothill, also earned a sharp rebuke in the course of the public debate. In his annual report he wrote:

> Reference to the vital statistics shows that the number of known illegitimate births has increased materially, and I have had reports that even a few married women are being somewhat more promiscuous than usual.

That much was undeniable, but he then added his view that:

> This is not surprising in view of the agencies at work tending to break up family and home life, such as the employment of women, nursery schools and classes, and communal feeding.

The chairman of the Education Committee protested at the inclusion of these personal views, and the City Council passed a resolution strongly disapproving of the paragraph.

So what was to be done? In Bury St Edmunds steps had already been taken during 1942 to supplement the work of the YWCA and the YMCA by opening a "Moral Welfare Home" for girls. Its limitations were described by a Bury diarist:

> It certainly is a "shelter", but, apart from domestic work, there is nothing except knitting for the girls to do. The library might fetch three shillings in a sale, and there isn't a table big enough even for table tennis. The staff usually play cards with them in the evening, or play the piano for the girls to sing. Once or twice a week there is a little church service in the small chapel upstairs. They now have an Ascot heater to provide hot water from the taps in the scullery, where the girls do their washing for themselves and babies, so it will no longer be necessary for them to draw water in buckets from the kitchen tap, and heat it in a copper.[10]

Lowestoft was exceptional in that it had appointed, in November, 1942, a trained woman moral welfare officer. In her first six months she helped thirty-two women and girls and made 214 visits, but she then left her post.

Something more was clearly necessary. The Church organised a "Religion and Life" week in Ipswich in September which attracted large audiences to hear talks by distinguished churchmen and women, including the Archbishop of Canterbury. The East Suffolk Probation Committee decided that it would "mention" its problems to the Home Office. Bury St Edmunds set up a Social Problems Committee. The minutes of a meeting of its ten ladies held in the Mayor's Parlour on 15th September indicate the main concerns but also the oblique language with which they were addressed:

> The Mayoress spoke of "difficult problems that had arisen in the borough owing to war time conditions".
> One speaker suggested talks to girls in the schools and youth organisations by GPs, and also the formation of a large and ambitious girls' club, where girls could come in and out, without membership rules and regulations.
> Another speaker suggested that the Vigilance Society could be approached with a view to a worker being sent to Bury station for a month or so, to try and stop the arrival of undesirable girls in the town . . . to pick out and question doubtful arrivals.

The committee adopted these suggestions, and also called for women police who could visit hotels and pubs nightly to inspect the identity cards of all suspected to be under sixteen, with instructions to send them home, and for a guild or club "to help the young wives of men overseas to find interests to help them overcome the loneliness and anxiety of their enforced separation"[11]. This was one of many such meetings. After another, at County Hall, a member of the council staff who attended noted in her diary:

> There was a meeting this afternoon about Americans, Blacks and other troops. Many clergy from different parts were there, also women speakers. It is considered that ten times as many girls will need rescue homes during the next three months. One speaker reported that in her district the black men were the biggest attraction and even bus-loads of married women came in to walk and lie down with them. It is thought it may be possible to get a ruling for Yanks to be in by 11 pm. It was said our police are not allowed to control the Yanks, or to say anything to them. The meeting is making another try to get women police here to look after the girls . . .[12]

Leaving this meeting and walking home through the blacked-out town the diarist experienced a sudden revelation of another aspect of the problems:

> As I came by the Corn Exchange there was a dance band playing and in a way I could understand young girls being attracted by the troops, like moths to a light; and one can understand the men, whose lower instincts have been roused to carry out their job in the war . . .

The Mayor of Bury St Edmunds tried moral exhortation, publishing an Open Letter to his citizens:

> It is our duty, to the best of our ability, so to lead our lives that our men and women folk serving away from home need have no unnecessary family worries and anxieties. So we ask ourselves: Is all well with us here in Bury St Edmunds? Is all well with our homes? Are they all still the kind of homes our men are thinking of, and to which they hope to return? Are we all endeavouring to do our duty in all ways which come to us? Are all wives conducting their homes in the way their husbands would expect? Are all mothers keeping that watchful eye on their children which is so necessary if they are to be brought up as their fathers would wish? Are all children and young people, especially those reaching the age of maturity, leading their lives in such a way that their fathers will be proud of them when they return?

On 21st November, 1943, the Parliamentary Secretary to the Ministry of Health, Miss Florence Horsbrugh, visited Bury St Edmunds to address a Sunday afternoon meeting in Bostock's Cinema, called by the Mayor to discuss "some serious moral problems". They had been wrong, she declared, not to tell boys and girls frankly about venereal disease.

A number of practical schemes were at last in train. Mrs Elaine Herbert, wife of the Bishop of Norwich, headed a committee of the Diocesan Council for Moral Welfare which opened "a home for unmarried mothers and their babies, for the accommodation of girls from the Services, NAAFI, the Land Army and ordinary civilian life". The Chief Constable of Norwich, Mr J. H. Dain, initiated a special campaign to stop the supply of intoxicating liquor to young persons under eighteen.

Throughout the year, at every stage in the discussion of the problems and how they might be ameliorated, one proposal was heard from all sides: that women police should be appointed in areas where there were concentrations of troops. No such appointments were made during 1943. Cambridge and Ipswich each had a few policewomen, and everyone agreed that their work was valuable. Cambridge had had them since 1916; and the four on the strength in 1943 patrolled the streets both day and night, visited cinemas and dance halls, and in general dealt chiefly with crimes affecting families. The Chief Constable, Mr R. J. Pearson, declared in August that their mere presence had had a sobering effect on the young and adolescent girls who congregated in the neighbourhood of military camps.

Early in January the Member of Parliament for Maldon, Mr Tom Driberg, called the attention of the Home Secretary to "the recent decision of the Essex Standing Joint Committee to shelve for two years the question of the appointment of policewomen in Essex". Mr Herbert Morrison made it clear that he wanted to encourage such appointments, and soon afterwards he formally advised police authorities to consider making them as a matter of urgency.

The West Suffolk Standing Joint Committee in July, 1943, voted 15–14 to defeat a proposal to employ policewomen: two in Bury, two in Newmarket, two in Sudbury, and one at headquarters. They would have been paid £2 17s a week and the cost would have been met by a government grant. The Chief Constable, Major Robertson, assured the committee he was not opposed to women police as such, but he said there were no vacancies in the force. Was there urgency such as to call for such an experiment in West Suffolk at that time, he inquired, adding: "Undoubtedly, young men and women behave in the streets in a manner to be deprecated, and in a way that shocks the older generation. But does that produce a criminal offence?" He wanted a clearer distinction between police duty and moral welfare, and argued that moral influence be exerted in the home.

Opponents of the appointments argued that the social problems were being exaggerated. "There is far too much tittle-tattle by Victorians of what they hold to be loose conduct," declared one. There might be some "skylarking", said another, but a good welfare officer could do more good in a talk with a mother than could a policewoman. That was also the view of Lord Bristol, who offered the revealing thought that welfare work would achieve comparable results "instead of upsetting the whole of the police force". So the West Suffolk legislators decided there would be no policewomen in their territory.

It was not a popular decision. Representatives from organisations in the town and villages within a ten-mile radius of Bury St Edmunds met in private on 31st August, under the chairmanship of the Mayor, to register their dismay. They asked the Standing Joint Committee to reconsider its decision. The committee was not pleased. When it met on 18th October it voted by 11 to 6 to inform the petitioners that it had already discussed and settled the matter, and did not see its way to reopen the subject. One member likened the petitioners to "the irresponsible public who are shouting for a second front".

Other East Anglian police authorities showed similar lack of enthusiasm. East Suffolk Standing Joint Committee actually decided to appoint two sergeants and nine constables "if possible": one sergeant at headquarters and one at Lowestoft, two constables to cover Stowmarket, Needham Market and Eye, two for Woodbridge, Saxmundham, Felixstowe, Aldeburgh and Leiston, two for Beccles, Bungay, Halesworth and Southwold, and three at Lowestoft. But when the year ended there was no sign of any of them.

The clamour for women police was maintained. An *Eastern Daily Press* leader in October asked for immediate appointments. The Norfolk and Norwich Council of Women urged "the appointment of trained and uniformed women police for the city". The Norfolk Federation of Women's Institutes and several rural district councils supported the call. The Bishop of Chelmsford wanted policewomen to drop into pubs to see what was going on, with a curfew for girls under eighteen and a "no treating" order. The Dowager Countess of Cranbrook, a member of the East Suffolk Probation Committee, identified herself with these demands at its December meeting, but observed sadly that the Standing Joint Committee had rejected the idea. The clerk told her that opposition to women police appeared to be "dying down", but the difficulty was to find suitable recruits.

There can be no doubt that male resistance to a wider role for women in the world of work was particularly strong in East Anglia. It was strong in the police force, and strong among farmers, who, as we have seen, were accepting land girls reluctantly. There was much other evidence. Fakenham magistrates, for example, were asked to renew the licences for two cinemas in the town with a woman as manager of the company which owned them. She had been with the company for eleven years; she told the magistrates that she had "never experienced any difficulty which the presence of a man would have eased"; there was no suggestion that the cinemas had been conducted other than to complete satisfaction. The magistrates decided they would renew the licences only if a male were appointed manager.

Women were expected to fill the ranks as voluntary workers in church, welfare and social service organisations, where they worked hard, but these organisations could only ameliorate a little the problems of under-age drinking, sexual permissiveness and child neglect.

The real scale of these social problems was never publicly defined—certainly no statistics were made available—and awareness of them varied greatly according to individual experience. The great majority of women worked hard, spent the hours of blackout in their own homes, and did their best to preserve the stability of family relationships. Among those of both sexes who had to be out and about at all hours there were many who chose not to see what was happening. Too open a discussion of the problems could be construed as unpatriotic behaviour, because it might cause "alarm and despondency", which was a punishable offence.

Perhaps it was in the nature of the war situation that nothing more could be done. Realists understood that the exceptional conditions under which people were living inevitably created acute social problems. The successful prosecution of the war was the paramount consideration. Any necessary price had to be paid.

CHAPTER TEN

Preparing for D-Day

THE FATEFUL day was drawing closer, the day that was to purge the nation of its consciousness of past failure and frustration, the day of action that would turn the tide of war and lead to victory. It was a day illumined in countless minds with a glow of hope; but it was also a day shadowed by dread of the price that would have to be paid. The prevailing public attitude was one of "Let's get on with it, and get it over as quickly as possible."

For those responsible for the conduct of the war it was not as simple as that. They had been under constant pressure from their Soviet Allies (and from Communist Party propagandists in the factories of Britain) to open a Second Front in Europe; but as 1943 began they still lacked the resources to undertake such a project. It had long been in the planning stage.

When Prime Minister Churchill and President Roosevelt met for a ten-day conference in Casablanca in the second half of January they already knew that "Overlord"—codename for the liberation of France—was not possible until 1944, and their communiqué merely promised "the assembly of the strongest possible force in constant readiness to re-enter the Continent as soon as German resistance is weakened to the required extent".[1]

Assembling a force of sufficient strength was not going to be easy. There were acute shortages in almost every area. Call-up to the Army during the period April to August was expected to be about 220,000, but normal wastage and battle casualties were estimated at 155,000 during the same period[2]. Many more landing craft were necessary, most of which would have to be built in and brought from shipyards in the United States. Operations in the Mediterranean and the Far East exercised conflicting claims; in particular, landing craft were being sent in large numbers for the invasion of Italy. On 15th April Churchill bluntly stated the position:

> We must recognise the fact that no important cross-Channel enterprise is possible this year. This is the fact which dominates action.

But he called for the immediate build-up of a Second Army of six divisions, to be trained and available for overseas action. Meanwhile, the weakness of the Allied position should be concealed from the enemy by

> . . . powerful camouflage and cover operations [which] should continue in order to pin the enemy to the French coast and not to discourage our Russian Allies . . . Very large preparations should be made at the embarkation ports, and the assembly of the greatest amount of barges and invasion craft should be made, culminating in July and August.[3]

145

Proposals for what the Combined Chiefs of Staff called "a full-scale assault against continental Europe" were prepared in August and were accepted by a conference of British and American defence staffs in Quebec the same month. They fixed 1st May, 1944, as a target date, but resolved:

> Balanced ground and air force to be built up for "Overlord" and there will be continuous planning for and maintenance of those forces available in the UK, in readiness to take advantage of any situation permitting an opportunistic cross-Channel move into France.[4]

Almost immediately afterwards, however, this plan was revised. It was agreed that five instead of three divisions would invade and that they would require more landing craft; so the date was postponed to June, 1944. At this stage, with the size of the expedition determined and a date in mind, it was possible to go ahead with the intensive inter-Service training that was called for. Churchill had created a new post of Director (later Chief) of Combined Operations back in June, 1940, and by the summer of 1943 Combined Operations bases and training establishments were springing up all round the coasts of the United Kingdom. Officers of all three

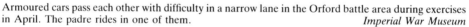

Armoured cars pass each other with difficulty in a narrow lane in the Orford battle area during exercises in April. The padre rides in one of them.   *Imperial War Museum*

services joined new staffs, new and strange types of vessels appeared, and "DD" tanks which could "swim" ashore from the vessels came forward from the factories.

Much planning was called for. There was hardly enough space to deploy the great forces involved. American troops were expected to arrive later in the year, and it was decided to base them in the south-west of England, while the British occupied the south-east and East Anglia. One British division, with its naval counterpart, was to do all its earlier training in the Moray Firth area in Scotland.

A large part of the coastal area of East Anglia was transformed into a training area. During 1942 an area of about 9,000 acres behind Orford Ness had been requisitioned as a battle area and 450 residents had been banished from their homes. Now more land was needed. In August General J. A. H. Gammell, GOC-in-C Eastern Command, had the difficult task of explaining to a further eighty-five people, working on five farms, that they must uproot themselves and leave, as their land was essential for an additional battle training school. Search had been made from the Wash to the Thames, he said, to find the area where least disturbance would be caused.

When the Army sought to requisition Fritton Decoy, a secluded lake near Lowestoft, however, for "tank training of a most secret nature", it met with difficulties. This had been a pleasure boating lake before the war and it was still used in 1943 as a highly organised duck shoot. Only a few people lived within the area the Army sought, but one of them was a peer of the realm with excellent contacts in Whitehall. On the day after a meeting took place in Cambridge between Army representatives, the Deputy Regional Commissioner, and other interested parties, the Under-Secretary of State at the War Office, Lord Croft, wrote this memorandum to the officer handling the matter:

> Lord K—— called to see me this morning. Unfortunately, Lady K—— is in a very dangerous state of health and he is convinced that he cannot move her without danger to her life. His physicians, Horder and Blake, would, he is sure, support this view. No-one, not even Lady K——, is aware of her condition—only Lord K—— and the physicians realise how serious is her state . . .
>
> I would remind you that he is a very distinguished servant of the Crown and a Privy Councillor, and I feel that if any possible adjustment can be made, he is a man whose honour and integrity to observe the utmost secrecy is beyond doubt.

Ten days later it was decided that civilians need not be evacuated from the area[5].

Among coastal areas requisitioned was one just north of Southwold, from below Covehithe village down to Easton Bavents, including Easton Broad, a farm and five cottages; this was used for Combined Assault Training. The removal of defensive minefields which had been laid during the days when a German invasion had been feared now proved a difficult task, here and elsewhere along the coast. After weeks of orthodox minesweeping, it was decided to run Churchill tanks up and down the beaches to explode any mines which had been missed[6].

It was also decided to leave in place the tubular scaffolding, tank ditches, pill-boxes and wire fences, "since it merely adds to the difficulties of landing and its negotiation is good practice for assaulting troops"[7]. Thus, formidable defences which had been erected by British troops in 1940 to give a hard time to Germans (who did not come) served in 1944 to toughen and train British invasion forces.

Southwold north beach, the North Denes beach at Great Yarmouth, and Gorleston and Landguard beaches were among others used for practice in landing men and vehicles from naval ships and craft. Something of the difficulty in clearing them of mines was explained in a memorandum written by the Chief Engineer of Eastern Command. At Yarmouth, he wrote, the number of mines recovered varied from thirty per cent to only one per cent of those that had been recorded. Gales and sea action meant that many were well below high water mark.

> The change of wind from north-east to south-east caused one tide to reveal nine mines on a swept beach, to be followed by a further two on the next tide.[8]

By September, 1943, East Anglia was packed with troops. Of the Home Forces, the 9th Armoured Division was around King's Lynn and Thetford and the 30th Armoured Brigade north of Newmarket. There was a very heavy concentration of forces in the Aldeburgh area. Of the 21st Army Group, in training for D-Day, the 1st Assault Division was around Yarmouth and Southwold, the 43rd Infantry Division in the Bury St Edmunds–Cambridge area, the 77th AA Brigade in the Peterborough–Kettering area, large numbers of other troops around Colchester and Chelmsford, a Dutch contingent at Harwich, and a Belgian contingent at Lowestoft[9]. There was much movement of Army units, but the general trend was to bring ever more troops into the region.

In December the 49th Division moved from Scotland to Eastern Command, making its headquarters at Sprowston Hall, Norwich, and sending Brigade Groups in turn to train at Studland Bay in Dorset. The 50th Division returned from overseas and moved into the Newmarket area, and the 76th Division was moved from the Ayrshire coast to the Norwich area[10]. The 79th Armoured Division was using the Orford and Dunwich Battle Area and other 21st Army Group troops were in the Southwold Assault Training Area, around Easton Broad. On the Norfolk Broads and along the coast preliminary training took place with the "DD" amphibious tanks, including instruction in launching and manoeuvring them in both fresh and salt water.

With so much going on, security measures were strict. At times mail posted in East Anglia was subject to censorship, and that was how a WAAF stationed at an RAF experimental station in the region found herself before a court that sat *in camera* in May. She had written a letter to her old headmistress, said the prosecution, giving "information of a highly secret character . . . which would undoubtedly be of great use to an enemy". Her letter had been intercepted. She was bound over for three years. Efforts were still made to deter visitors to the

An Airspeed Horsa glider built for airborne operations. Many hundreds of them were assembled at bomber airfields in eastern England.   *British Aircraft Corporation*

region, but many day-trippers turned up during the bright, hot summer. The Southend Residents' Association complained to the Regional Commissioner and asked him to consider re-imposing an absolute ban. On one day in July, they asserted, 16,000 visitors were admitted to the town, with the consequence that they had been unable to get their allotted food rations[11].

Although security had to be safeguarded, the authorities did not actually want to conceal the scale of the invasion preparations. The activity in East Anglia was serious training for some of the forces that would be engaged in the coming invasion. The naval assault force, when D-Day arrived, would be held in harbours from Harwich to the south[12] and troops would embark in ports from Felixstowe on the east coast right round to the Bristol Channel; shipping was to be brought coastwise in convoy to a rendezvous near the Isle of Wight.

Likewise, minesweepers from the east coast ports would be among the twenty-nine flotillas which would sweep channels through enemy minefields so that the assault convoys could go through. All this had to be well prepared.

Horsa gliders which airborne troops would use were made ready in such quantities that their storage posed a problem. Many hundreds of them were assembled at bomber airfields in the eastern counties, including Downham Market, Methwold and Sculthorpe.

This activity, despite its serious purpose, embraced a major exercise in deception. The Allied invasion troops were to sail from the south coast and land in

149

Normandy, but the C-in-C of 21st Army Group in East Anglia was made responsible for planning, preparing and executing an elaborate "cover" plan:

> . . . to induce the enemy to believe that the main assault and follow-up will be in or east of the Pas de Calais area, thereby encouraging the enemy to maintain or increase the strength of his air and ground forces and of his fortifications there, at the expense of other areas . . .
>
>   to keep the enemy in doubt as to the date and time of the actual assault . . .
>
>   during and after the main assault to contain the largest possible German ground and air forces on or east of the Pas de Calais area for at least 14 days.

General Gammell, GOC-in-C of Eastern Command, was told that:

> Orders should, whenever possible, make no distinction between the aspects of the real and cover operations . . . The deceptive aspect of the cover operation will be divulged to as few as possible.[13]

Meanwhile during the summer of 1943 the RAF was being reorganised for the tasks ahead. Hitherto, much of its effort had been to combat attacks on Britain; now it was being transformed into an offensive force.

Part of Fighter Command continued to be responsible for the air defence of Great Britain, but fighter aircraft that had previously supported Bomber Command were formed into the 2nd Tactical Air Force, which was to prepare the way into France for the Army and then to give it very close support. Its more immediate task was to make low-level attacks on targets such as railway yards and power stations, generally to harass the enemy on the ground, to entice German fighters to battle in the hope of destroying as many of them as possible, and to deter the Luftwaffe from renewing daylight attacks on Britain. The new C-in-C, Air Vice-Marshal Basil Embry, set up his headquarters in Bylaugh Hall, a large country mansion seven miles from East Dereham, and immediately began to plan for the invasion[14]. Every day the people of East Anglia watched the planes of this new force crossing the North Sea coast.

The Americans, too, began to create a new air force to provide tactical support for the coming invasion, the Ninth USAAF, and by the end of the year its strength was being built up on East Anglian bases. When Raydon airfield was opened in December it was immediately assigned to the Ninth Air Force, 357th Fighter Group, and there was an influx of pilots during December and a great deal of training.

The RAF Tactical Air Force played its part in the Great Deception when it took part in a simulated invasion operation codenamed "Starkey" in September. The RAF planes made an onslaught on airfields and military targets in France, and at the same time numbers of troops, transports and assault craft were concentrated in the UK. The climax was on 9th September, when assault and landing craft actually sailed from Kent ports, escorted by naval craft, and headed towards Boulogne. This big combined operation was designed to bring the Luftwaffe to large-scale battle and to force it to bring back units from Italy.

At about this same time the 7th Battalion of the Royal Norfolk Regiment, which had spent the summer under canvas at Northiam, in Kent, was preparing for its role in the invasion. It was part of the 59th Division, which had joined the 12th Corps as a follow-up division to go ashore after the initial landings. Now it took part in a large-scale exercise to test the administrative organisation and the marshalling arrangements that would be required on and after D-Day. On this occasion the Norfolk men did not get beyond the quay at Dover; afterwards they moved into winter quarters in Margate.

Most battalions of the East Anglian regiments found their duties now geared to the planning for the invasion, but their experiences varied greatly. The 1st Royal Norfolks and the 1st Suffolks, who were part of the 3rd Division, had been assigned a principal role. When the first broad plan for the invasion was completed, the 3rd Division was named as one of the three divisions which would go ashore first, the others being American and Canadian. (Later two more divisions were added, one British and one American). The 3rd Division's training earlier in the year had given clear indication of its likely employment as an assault force. The Royal Norfolks had spent the first few months in Yorkshire and Northumberland, where their arduous routine had included four-day exercises, marching thirty miles a day through hill country with full equipment and stores carried on a man-pack basis, sleeping in the open at night, and undergoing mock attacks by the RAF. The 1st Suffolks had spent a good deal of 1942 in Scotland, practising embarking and disembarking on an open coast, and had then moved down to Folkestone, where they were equipped with six-pounder anti-tank guns. They suffered numerous drafts for overseas service, some men being sent to India and a contingent of seventy to the Mediterranean, where later they fought together on the Anzio beachhead.

The 3rd Division moved to the Scottish Highlands during May, 1943, and both the 1st Royal Norfolks and the 1st Suffolks joined with naval forces to rehearse beach landings from the lochs. There was continuous practice in embarking and disembarking, day and night, first in platoons, finally in brigades. The officers began to think that they would be in action long before D-Day, and looked to the Mediterranean theatre, but the division was still in Scotland when the invasion of Sicily took place on 20th July. The assault training continued in several parts of the Highlands, with "battle inoculation" exercises in which concealed charges were detonated and live ammunition and mortar bombs were fired over companies. "The Division trained as never an infantry division trained before," its historian wrote afterwards[15].

The 1st Suffolks moved to the Western Highlands in June for an intensive toughening course, including several assault landings using live ammunition. Everyone then spent several days at a Divisional Battle School at Moffat learning the techniques of assaulting strong points and how to "open up" steel and concrete bunkers and pillboxes surrounded by wire and mines; after that during August there was "group training", with Churchill tanks, machine-guns, and small landing craft. Live ammunition and explosives were used in all these exercises. In October the 1st Suffolks moved to Pembrokeshire, where they trained with an armoured division, and after that returned to Scotland, to the Invergordon area, to link up with the Navy. The whole of the 3rd Division went to sea in newly-arrived LSIs (Landing Ships, Infantry)—American ships of about 11,000 tons carrying eighteen LCAs (Landing Craft, Assault), each of which was designed to carry thirty-five men. The Merchant Navy manned the LSIs, and the LCAs were crewed by Marines.

Towards the end of the year companies of the 1st Norfolks were moved in rotation to Suffolk and attached to the 13th/18th Royal Hussars for training with tanks. In the D-Day plan, the 13th/18th Hussars had been assigned a special role: they were to take the plunge from an LCT 5,000 yards offshore and make for land in their amphibious Sherman tanks.

In December the whole of the 3rd Division was assembled, with headquarters at Inverness, for a full-scale rehearsal of D-Day. The planners had decided that the Moray Firth provided "a fair reproduction of the actual tides, beach, ridges and

A smoke screen is laid down during an Eastern Command exercise near Yarmouth in May.
Imperial War Museum

lateral roads likely to be encountered" in Normandy. The little Scottish town of Burghead found itself the objective as for the first time the whole process of the invasion was practised[16].

Another battalion of the Royal Norfolks, the 9th, provided parties from September, 1943, to assist with the running of a chain of camps along the south coast, part of the springboard on which the invasion troops were to be concentrated.

During this period of hectic activity there was debate about the use to be made of the Home Guard. Nationally there were now nearly two million men serving in it. The elderly and unfit had been weeded out, many of them going very unwillingly. The average age of the force had come down to a little under thirty[17]. This meant, of course, that they all were employed in jobs in industry or agriculture that were essential to the war effort, and the Prime Minister privately expressed concern in March that they were being asked to do too much, referring in a memorandum to several War Cabinet colleagues to "the very serious burden" involved in forty-eight hours' a month drill and sentry duty. "Whatever anyone may say, this extra duty is bound to reduce a man's output," he wrote, and he asked that commanders should be instructed not to insist on too many exhausting exercises and to release men in agricultural and industrial work[18].

Notwithstanding this, members of the Home Guard in East Anglia were prosecuted during the summer months if they missed parades, as were a number of men who refused to enrol.

But the Home Guard in the region was in good heart and at its peak strength—seventeen battalions in Norfolk. Although it paraded as usual, however, the dangers which had called the force into existence had clearly now receded. So was there another role for it?

During October there was discussion of the possibility that it might be mustered during the period of invasion of Europe (from D-Day minus two until D-Day plus ten) to serve in the assembly and transit areas where invasion troops would be concentrated. The idea was quickly dismissed, partly because of the effect on production in the factories and on the farms. A Home Forces GHQ order dated 2nd November decreed that Home Guards were to perform night duties only near their homes and for the normal maximum of forty-eight hours in every four weeks.

General Gammell in Eastern Command was one of those keen to muster the Home Guard, and he followed up the War Office order with one of his own in which he declared: "On psychological grounds, full mobilisation of the Home Guard in this Command would be a great tonic to the Home Guard in general. But, if this is considered undesirable, then full use of the Home Guard must be made by some other means."

He proposed that 6,300 Home Guard in Suffolk and Essex and 825 in Norfolk and Cambridgeshire should be asked to volunteer and should be used to "thicken up the defence . . ." He wanted to concentrate them at Harwich, Ipswich,

Felixstowe, Tilbury and the Blackwater hards, with units of 100 men at each of Yarmouth and Lowestoft for local defence and small groups guarding bridges, railway junctions and other vital points in Norfolk and Cambridgeshire[19]. "Exercises rehearsing the scheme should be carried out from time to time, and the final exercise should be the actual operation," the general proposed. This final exercise would begin on D minus seven. He thought the whole concept would assist the "cover plan" for which he was responsible.

Everyone's sight was now firmly fixed on the coming summer. Only a few knew when D-Day was likely, but everyone felt confident that it was coming close. This belief was confirmed on 27th December when it was announced that General Dwight Eisenhower had been appointed "Supreme Allied Commander of the British and US Expeditionary Force organising in the UK for the liberation of Europe". General Sir Bernard Montgomery was named as C-in-C of the British Group of Armies, under General Eisenhower; and General Spaatz to command the American Strategic Bombing Force operating against Germany. That same day Eisenhower declared his conviction that the Allies would win the European war during 1944.

Members of Horringer Home Guard pose outside the Rotunda at Ickworth during 1943.

CHAPTER ELEVEN

Looking for a New Dawn

DECISIONS about the conduct of the war to victory could be made only by the War Cabinet and the Service chiefs—everyone understood that. But decisions about the new society that was to be built after the war were *everyone's* business, and every Tom, D(a)i and Harriet was keen to offer a view. Public discussion and debate about post-war policies became an outstanding feature of life in 1943.

There had been much stimulus from official quarters. During the dog days of the war, while men and women in the armed Services and in Civil Defence had had perforce to sit and wait, discussion groups had been encouraged in order to sustain morale. The Army had had its Bureau of Current Affairs, organising regular sessions in every unit, since the autumn of 1941. Cambridge University helped to educate some of the Education Officers charged with this task. In January, 1943, for example, fifty-five officers of Eastern and AA Commands attended a three-day course, the men going into residence at King's and Trinity and eight ATS officers at Newnham; later there were courses in Norwich and Cambridge for National Fire Service discussion leaders, who returned to their units to arrange current affairs classes and debates.

Among civilians, similar activity was set in train by a variety of organisations. The Cambridge branch of the Workers' Educational Association, for example, announced at the beginning of the year several twelve-session series of classes with titles such as "Some International Problems", "Architecture" and "The Social Services and Local Government".

These matters had ceased to be the province of "intellectuals" and were no longer concerned with abstract theory. Many characteristic features of pre-war British society had been denounced and discarded. With Victory must come A New Start. By the beginning of 1943 some began to wonder if the process was going too far and too fast. On 12th January the Prime Minister circulated a note to members of the Cabinet entitled "Promises about Post-War Conditions", the first sentence of which read: "A dangerous optimism is growing up about the conditions it will be possible to establish here after the war." Mr Churchill contrasted some of the promises that were being made with difficulties that the nation would confront after the war, such as the almost complete disappearence of her foreign investments. "Ministers should, in my view, be careful not to raise false hopes, as was done last time . . . It is because I do not wish to deceive the people by false hopes and airy visions of Utopia and Eldorado that I have refrained so far from making promises about the future," he wrote[1].

It was the government itself, however, which had opened up most areas of discussion, and never more boldly than when it had asked Sir William Beveridge to recommend how social welfare schemes should be financed after the war. The Beveridge Report, issued in December, 1942, immediately caught the public imagination and set off intense debate[2]. During the early months of 1943 there was scarcely a public figure or organisation in East Anglia remaining silent on the matter. The Cambridge branch of the National Council of Women petitioned local MPs with a resolution of support for the proposals. Cambridge students met at the Guildhall, heard speeches by Dr Edith Summerskill, MP, and Mr Peter Shore, chairman of the University Labour Club, and called on the government to implement the report "immediately". The Workers' Educational Association had economist Joan Robinson to take them through the report, and the Cambridge Women's Liberal Association formed a "Beveridge Study Group".

There was a similar ferment among the organisations in Norwich and Ipswich, and even the country towns joined in—the Guildhall in Bury St Edmunds was packed when a Labour *guru*, Professor Harold J. Laski, came to talk about Beveridge.

In February Winston Churchill wrote another memorandum to his Cabinet colleagues, specifically about the Beveridge Report. He thought its approach to social security was "an essential part of any post-war scheme of national betterment", and he proposed that a body should be set up to work until the war ended "polishing, reshaping, and preparing for the necessary legislation". But that legislation, and the commitment to the expenditure involved, would have to wait for "a responsible Government and a House of Commons refreshed by contact with the people"[3]. A two-day debate took place in the Commons in February, when Sir John Anderson asserted that the government wished to follow the general lines of development of the social services laid down in the report, but added that that did not mean that all the main features of the report commended themselves equally. Labour found this unsatisfactory and moved an amendment urging early implementation of the Beveridge Plan, but this was defeated by 335 votes to 119.

The Beveridge debate went on throughout 1943. Sir William himself spoke in Cambridge Guildhall in November on "The Meaning and Price of Social Security", insisting there was nothing unworkable in his plan. The most remarkable thing he said was that he had received no communication from the government during the year since the report had been published.

In one area of reform, education, the government had decided to press ahead immediately with legislation. An East Anglian MP, Mr R. A. Butler, was the Minister entrusted with the task, and he told a Chelmsford audience early in the year that the objective he had in mind was "not exactly equality, but equivalent dignity to all children". He explained: "What we can attempt to ensure is that each child gets an equal choice and chance, so that they can have training suitable for their talents." That would mean, for older children, that there would be secondary, technical and senior schools.

His Education Bill appeared in December and specified that the school-leaving age would be raised to fifteen on 1st April, 1945, and further increased to sixteen "directly the Minister is satisfied that this is practicable"—which meant as soon as teachers and buildings were available. Later, young people up to eighteen years of age would have to attend Young People's Colleges for one day a week, for forty-four weeks each year, or for an equivalent period of time. The existing division of education into elementary and higher phases was to be replaced by "a continuous process conducted in three successive stages—primary, secondary, and further". The Minister called it "the most comprehensive measure in the history of English and Welsh education".

Beveridge was one among a number of individuals and committees invited by the government to propose post-war policies, and their reports were now dropping on to Whitehall desks and feeding the public appetite for reform. The Rushcliffe Report in February set out a new deal for the nursing profession, with a proper salary structure and defined holidays and working conditions for the first time in the history of nursing. A state registered nurse, it proposed, should receive a salary of £70 a year, plus emoluments, to make a total of between £115 and £145.

Army officers and NCOs and WRNS officers attend an educational course in the Pier Pavilion at Felixstowe in May. It was at such courses that "post-war conditions" were discussed.

Imperial War Museum

Proposals of special interest to the eastern counties were offered in the Scott Report, which put forward a body of principles for the planning of housing and services in rural areas. West Suffolk County Council called a meeting of local authority delegates to discuss town and country planning and resolved to create a West Suffolk Joint Planning Committee, to which should be delegated all the local authority's powers other than that to levy a rate or to borrow money. The new committee would exercise control over the use of land, density of building and the external appearance of buildings.

The County Councils' Association published proposals for reform which envisaged larger local government areas. The *Eastern Daily Press*, in an editorial comment, gave them a guarded welcome:

> . . . based upon the contention that small areas have not the resources at their disposal for the really effective equipment and staffing of public services on the scale of modern requirements.

Although the paper went on to argue the importance of retaining "local spirit and local pride", its views were out of line with those of the men and women serving on local authorities at every level, county, town and district. All over East Anglia outraged opposition was heard: the general fear was that a trend towards centralisation was emerging. East Suffolk County Council declared that the County Councils' Association recommendations would involve doing away with the charters of four boroughs, Beccles, Southwold, Aldeburgh and Eye. There was spontaneous applause in the Council Chamber at Cambridge as a resolution was passed opposing the reform proposals. Its sponsor, Alderman W. L. Raynes, feared that "the general policy seems to be the establishment of regional services, and if there is one subject which is an anathema to local authorities of every kind it is the development of regionalism . . . with the control and settlement of policy divorced from us as representatives of the ratepayers of this borough". At Wymondham UDC the chairman, Mr E. G. Gooch, insisted that the proposals would abolish all the urban district councils and the town would be merged into the county.

The same danger of over-centralisation was detected in other proposals. Bury St Edmunds Town Council, for example, "viewed with great apprehension" the idea that control of maternity and child welfare should be handed over to the county councils, the Mayor claiming that these services had been dealt with on progressive lines and with efficiency, whereas transfer to the county council would so increase bureaucracy as to prove catastrophic. The same council was concerned that education and hospitals might be lost to local administration.

No subject aroused more discussion and controversy than housing. German explosives had destroyed or severely damaged hundreds of thousands of homes and gutted whole town centres, and East Anglia had suffered its share of these losses.

Additionally, many pre-war homes that had survived in the backstreets of Ipswich, Norwich, Cambridge and most other towns, and in the rural villages as well, were below the standard which would be acceptable when the war was over. Again, the government encouraged the popular aspirations. The Minister of Health, Mr Ernest Brown, said during March that Britain might need three to four million new homes after the war, adding:

> In order to get the wheel turning immediately the war ends—or sooner, if conditions permit—there is much thinking and planning to be done. My Ministry and the Central Housing Advisory Committee are hard at work on questions of design, standards of construction, equipment and rural housing.

There was immediate and urgent need for more houses for the families of men working in agriculture, and the Minister announced that three thousand would be built forthwith, saying that this would be "in the nature of a commando raid, from which we shall gain experience". They would also aim, in conjunction with the local authorities and the Ministry of Works, to repair before the end of the year forty thousand houses which had been seriously damaged and were still unoccupiable. "I can hold out no hope of other new house-building for the time being," he added. The eastern counties were to have many of the new council houses for farm workers: Lincolnshire 228, Norfolk 90, Suffolk 72, Essex 66, and Cambridgeshire, Huntingdonshire and the Isle of Ely 26 each. Melford RDC was the first council in the region to start work on them—six at Stoke-by-Nayland. A few weeks later building was also going on at Rougham, Bardwell, Great Ashfield and Drinkstone. By mid-November the Minister of Health was able to announce that 2,260 were under construction.

Long before then the scheme was under fierce attack. About a third of the new houses were to be flat-roofed, and this design proved unpopular. A member of the East Suffolk Public Health Committee declared they were "totally unsuitable for their requirements". The flat roofs were unsatisfactory, and because the houses were built of cement they would be cold in winter and uncomfortably hot in summer. For good measure, he added that the rents of ten to thirteen shillings a week would be beyond the means of families who were living in tied cottages on the farms at three shillings a week. "Nobody likes them and nobody wants them," he assured a meeting of the Health Committee.

Blyth RDC went further, suspending all plans to build the homes until a special committee had met the Regional Architect to try to persuade him that they "would be totally unsuitable for rural districts and always a disgrace to the county". The council's surveyor declared that roof joists of those with pitched roofs would be inadequate to carry pantiles, and that an upstairs room which was called a bathroom, against a day when piped water might be available, was useless meanwhile as a bedroom, while tenants would have to bath downstairs. An architect member of the council said the house had been designed for suburban areas, where there was a piped water supply and sewerage. What was wanted in the country was a wash-house. The surveyor wryly summed up: "I hope the council will not think the plans are my brainstorm."

Even before this criticism was raised in the villages, the hapless Minister was being vigorously attacked at Westminster by an erstwhile colleague. Lord Beaverbrook, who less than a year before had been a member of the Cabinet, told the House of Lords that the minimum number of agricultural cottages required immediately was not three thousand but thirty thousand. He declared that a bureaucratic machine to produce these houses had been built up much faster than the houses would be built. Norfolk was to get ninety houses, and it was considered necessary for eleven different authorities there to consider the matter and for farmers who were involved to deal with 111 rules and orders from the Ministry of Agriculture. Lord Portal, who replied for the government, said there was only enough labour and materials to build three thousand. More than four hundred hostels for land girls and camps for prisoners of war had to be built at the same time.

This argument did not deter local authorities who wanted to plan the new housing they would require when the war ended. Cambridge Housing Committee set a target of three hundred new houses in the first year of peace, and a post-war ten-year programme of 4,500 to 5,000 houses divided between council and private enterprise properties. It sought Ministry approval to proceed immediately with the purchase of 400 acres of land.

The scale of other towns' ambitions is suggested by King's Lynn's scheme for nearly nine hundred houses and flats (including the £1 million Gaywood Hall Estate, with 562 homes), Colchester's target of 444 houses in the first year, and Newmarket's desire for a hundred. Only Southwold Town Council announced that it wanted no new working-class dwellings after the war, which the *East Anglian Daily Times* pronounced "a unique decision".

Great Yarmouth and Lowestoft, which had lost large numbers of houses in the raids, were ambitious to replace them. Great Yarmouth Town Council approved a scheme in February to provide sites for 1,500 houses in the immediate post-war year, and then for a thousand each year for ten years. Lowestoft Town Council decided in April that it would need six hundred new houses in the first post-war year, on the assumption that private enterprise would build a further hundred. Officials of both councils were called to the Ministry of Health and told that such large numbers were not practical propositions. Great Yarmouth had to scale down its programme to 350 houses during the first post-war year, Lowestoft to three hundred.

Most towns in East Anglia did not restrict their post-war planning to domestic dwellings. Particularly where town centres had been bombed, they now aspired to replace them with showpiece buildings. Great Yarmouth, for example, drafted a programme of post-war improvements which included a conference hall in the town

The aftermath of an air raid on Norwich in March in which a clothing factory was destroyed. Such destruction gave the opportunity for drawing up new development plans.   *George Swain*

centre, extension and improvement of the Wellington Pier, and larger ornamental gardens.

Norwich City Council appointed a London town planning consultant, Mr F. Longstreth Thompson, and two architectural advisors to prepare a complete development plan for the city, to be ready within twelve months. Working with the City Engineer and the City Architect, they were to produce proposals for "a beautiful and convenient city", taking account of realignment of principal roads, location of industry, and the future of the cattle market. The council had earlier run into controversy when it suggested the cattle market should be removed to the Harford Estate*.

Coastal towns foresaw that they would face special problems when the war ended and representatives of Chambers of Commerce from twelve east and south coast resorts met in London in October to emphasise their "acute financial problems". They formed a Coastal Resorts Distress Committee and urged the Ministry of Health to give preliminary thought to rapid restoration of hotels, boarding houses, catering establishments and other facilities immediately hostilities ended. Southend, Harwich, Lowestoft and Great Yarmouth were represented on

*Notwithstanding the strong objections of farmers, the city council did remove the cattle market to a new site after the war.

this committee, which presented a case that the whole nation should share the financial burden in these defence and evacuation areas. The Town Clerk of Lowestoft said: "The government should be asked, among other things, to remove defence works on the beaches as soon as possible after the war, and to give priority release of requisitioned property to the hotel and catering industry."

The east coast local authorities were also greatly concerned about the state of their sea defences, insisting that the repairs necessary could not be delayed until after the war. Lowestoft's Mayor, Major S. W. Humphery, accused government departments of "lamentable" delays. At Pakefield during the early part of 1943 high tides and a heavy swell scoured large areas of cliffs and the sea reached the ancient churchyard. The church itself had been gutted by incendiary bombs in April, 1941, and now a corner of the churchyard, with its enclosing wall, tumbled down to the beach.

No-one voiced more concern about the post-war prospects than the farmers and farmworkers. The employers' apprehensions were three-fold: they were worried about the long-term consequences of taking fertility out of the soil in order to boost food production during the war; they were worried about their financial future, as determined by farm prices fixed by the government; and they were worried about the degree of post-war control of their activities. The chairman of the Suffolk NFU, Mr Makens Turner, voiced the first fear. They were "whipping" the land and mortgaging the future, he declared. That being so, the profits that arose were largely paper profits. Throughout 1943 farming spokesmen, and especially "Lavengro", the farm correspondent writing in the *East Anglian Daily Times*, urged the need for more manuring, but the Ministry of Agriculture was not impressed. The Minister, Mr R. S. Hudson, told the Commons he was quite satisfied that official policy was not destroying the fertility of the soil. The Norfolk NFU Executive studied this speech and expressed deep concern, every speaker rejecting the Minister's view, and one warning that they were creating a danger of dust bowls, as in the United States.

The chairman of the Norfolk NFU, Mr Alfred Lewis, was a spokesman on the second major anxiety, which was about farm prices. At the annual meeting early in the year, at which he took office, he warned:

We must be ever mindful that the industry has only received a pledge of price stability for one year after the war. Before the war closes, we shall need to be well equipped with an adequate and permanent post-war policy.

Mr Lewis also raised early in the year the other spectre that haunted farmers: central control of their activities.

While it is to be hoped that petty-fogging restrictions will be dispensed with at the earliest possible moment, it would be a grievous fault to clamour for complete decontrol immediately following the declaration of peace. A fixed price and a guaranteed market to enable the efficient farmer to produce the maximum capacity must remain their aim in the interim.

Yet when the national vice-president of the NFU later suggested that some controls must continue after the war, the Norfolk branch executive was up in arms, declaring that "to commit the NFU and farmers of the county to the continuance of bureaucratic and committee control after the war was going too far". The council of the NFU in London backed their vice-president, whose comments, they said, had reflected NFU council policy. The *East Anglian Daily Times* joined in the argument with a leading article:

> Farmers have been set on their feet, but those who have helped to establish them there seem to imagine they will promptly lose their equilibrium if the support of bureaucratic oversight were to be withdrawn. Not a few of our cultivators and raisers of stock, however, look forward to the relaxation of control and a return to individualistic farming . . .

That was all right with its readers; it echoed the feeling of most East Anglian farmers. But the article then went on:

> . . . it must be clear that, so long as the Exchequer helps to subsidise farming activities, some amount of direction, if not dictation, there must be.

A Newmarket farmer wrote to protest. As he saw things, the Exchequer was not subsidising activities; it was subsidising the nation as a whole by holding down the cost of living. "If farmers were allowed a free market for their produce, they would be receiving much more than the present controlled prices," he declared.

The newspaper's agricultural correspondent, "Lavengro", followed up his editor's leading article with a vague but gloomy prognostication:

> Ponder over the Minister of Agriculture's most recent remarks. Are they not indicative, to some extent, of the ultimate fate that awaits British agriculture, which, in the meantime, bureaucracy is bent on turning topsy-turvey? I may be wrong in saying that, in the end, farmers will be left to shift for themselves, but it looks uncommonly like happening.

When, towards the end of the year, the House of Lords discussed one specific problem of post-war agriculture—compensation for farmers whose land had been requisitioned for defence purposes—the vagueness of the government's attitude did nothing to assuage farmers' apprehensions. In the debate Lord Hastings cited an example of a trustee estate in East Anglia with an agricultural value of £20 an acre. If 700 acres were taken for an airfield, the owner might get £14,000 on derequisition, with the return of his land. But, Lord Hastings asserted, it might cost £40,000 to restore the land to its former use, when it would again be a property worth £14,000. What would the State have to say if trustees, in such circumstances, chose simply to invest the £14,000 and let the land go derelict? The Earl of Cranbrook said that in his part of East Anglia whole villages had been affected by land requisitioning. There would be compensation for the landlord, but the working people who had been displaced were looking forward to reinstatement. If this did not happen, they would get no compensation.

The Lord Chancellor told them the government could not decide at that time what was to be done in many of these cases—it would depend upon future agricultural and planning policy. He indicated that the War Agricultural Executive Committees might have a role in determining what would happen. If they considered that land should be restored to its former use in the national interest the government might consider whether the Crown should meet the cost of doing so. If no national interest required this, or if the expense would be out of all proportion to the injury done, the land might not be reinstated, but compensation would be paid.

The National Union of Agricultural Workers also felt it had reason to be anxious about the future, for, despite its fight for a £4 a week minimum wage, it was still far from achieving it, and its campaign on hours and holidays had not dented the fifty-hour week in the summer months. There were still only four days' paid holiday per year, and the Norfolk employers had just come up with a proposal to

A typical wartime scene in Suffolk: members of the Garrard family carting hay at Church Farm, Great Glemham. *Mrs Faith Garrard*

institute a new twelve to fourteen years old age group, with wages for both sexes of fivepence an hour. The gulf between farmers and workers was as wide as ever it had been.

The position of women in the post-war world was another subject of exploratory debate, and there were signs of a women's movement stirring. When the Cambridge and District Women Citizens' Association met in March its secretary observed that the war had interrupted its work of finding and putting forward women to serve on the different local authorities, and she added:

> The time has now arrived when thought should again be given to this activity, and the committee feel there must be many women who are now doing responsible war work who will be glad to have this opportunity for further service after the war.

The Cambridge Union Society, at about the same time, defeated a provocative motion "that the enfranchisement of women has led to the emasculation of British politics", but three months later, at a members' meeting, it declined to admit women students to associate membership. The motion was not voted down; instead, the house was counted out, for want of a quorum, although there were many members just outside the debating chamber.

The leader of one of Britain's biggest trade unions, with many women members, Mr Arthur Deakin, expressed his view that there would never be a return to "the old-time idea that a woman's place is in the home". The *East Anglian Daily Times* suggested editorially that he was "altogether wrong", and inquired: "what is considered the overriding gain in happiness to be substituted for the home and all its domestic machinery, which is the essential foundation of the life of the community?" It came to the conclusion that "women have not yet found a satisfactory substitute for child-bearing and rearing". The correspondence columns showed little evidence of a feminine backlash.

There was less debate about the nature of the post-war settlement with the enemy nations than there was about domestic policies, but the Labour Member of Parliament for Ipswich, Mr Richard Stokes, moved a resolution at the Labour Party's annual conference in London in June asserting that the best hope of destroying the aggressive forces in Germany, Italy and Japan and of establishing a just and lasting peace lay in eliminating "anti-social and militarist vested interests".

The resolution condemned what it called "the false identification of the peoples with vicious governments", opposed any idea of a treaty of revenge, and called for encouragement of socialist and democratic governments in the enemy countries. It was vigorously opposed by leaders of three of the biggest trade unions, whose attitude was expressed in an amendment declaring that "the Nazi government would not have remained in power or been able to conduct a total war but for the support it received from the overwhelming majority of the German People". Germany, they insisted, would have to be completely disarmed and the spirit of aggressive nationalism entirely eradicated. With the unions using their block votes, this view was accepted by the conference by 1,803,000 votes to 720,000.

Labour organisations in the country were as keen as the various special interest groups to insist on a bigger role in the post-war world, but they seemed less specific with their proposals. When the Cambridge Trades Council and Labour Party resumed the traditional May Day demonstration on Parker's Piece on 2nd May speakers stressed the demand that "a Labour government should make the peace", and at the Labour Party conference in London during June one of its best-known leaders, Mr Herbert Morrison, forecast "a terrific battle about the future of controls and of economic planning" after the war. If there was not proper planning, he declared, the country would have eighteen months' good time, with high wages and prices, followed by three or four years of slump and collapse. At the same conference the Party's leader, Mr Clement Attlee, promised that when hostilities with Germany ended, or when there was any question of a general election, the party conference would be asked to decide whether Labour should or should not continue to participate in government.

It would be a mistake to suppose that Prime Minister Winston Churchill, his energies so completely engaged in supervising the war effort, was opposed to this intense debate about post-war society. Indeed, he joined in.

A broadcast he made on Sunday, 21st March was hailed as the "first authoritative and comprehensive picture of Britain's post-war aims". When the fighting was over the United Nations, headed by the British Commonwealth, America and Russia, would immediately confer upon the future world organisation to prevent war, he said, and he visualised a "Council of Europe" (and another for Asia), with a High Court and with armed forces ready to enforce decisions. On the home front, there would have to be an early election. His suggestion was that a coalition government might announce a Four Year Plan for transition and reconstruction, including compulsory national insurance "from the cradle to the grave"; a new deal for agriculture; national public health services; broader and more liberal education, with equality of opportunity; replanned towns and cities; and a revival of industry, with an extension of state industry side by side with encouragement of private enterprise.

"I look forward to a Britain so big that she will need to draw her leaders from every type of school and wearing every kind of tie," he went on. "Tradition may play its part, but broader systems must now rule." Of industry, he said: "There is a broadening field for State ownership and enterprise, especially in relation to monopolies of all kinds. The modern State will increasingly concern itself with the economic well-being of the nation, but it is all the more vital to revive at the earliest moment a widespread, healthy and vigorous private enterprise, without which we shall never be able to provide in the years when it is needed the employment of our soldiers, sailors and airmen, to which they are entitled after their duty has been done."

He called on his forty years' experience in Parliament, and his twenty-five years in Cabinet, to underline his "solemn belief" that:

> If we act with comradeship and loyalty to our country and to one another, and if we can make State enterprise and free enterprise both serve national interests and pull the national waggon side by side, then there is no need for us to run into that horrible devastating slump or into that squalid epoch of bickering and confusion which mocked and squandered the hard-won victory which we gained a quarter of a century ago.

Few contributors to the debate had ranged more widely or sounded more radical than that. There were some public figures who strongly disapproved of all such talk. One was Mr J. Gibson Jarvie, of Gedding Hall, near Bury St Edmunds, a banker who as chairman of United Dominions Trust Ltd had made a national reputation as a right-wing economist. At a meeting of the Thameside Development Board, of which he was president, he attacked all planners, saying: "If some of these plans which are receiving favour today materialise, it will take this country a century of misery and frustration to retrieve the position, and only then to the role of a third-rate power, with the Empire and all it stands for broken up and disintegrated." Members of the Development Board formally dissociated themselves from these views, and Gibson Jarvie resigned. He was running against the tide of public opinion, a tide which Churchill understood.

Several by-elections occurred during 1943, and the pattern of voting gave the government cause for concern. Candidates who challenged the wartime compact and forced a poll concentrated not on criticism of the conduct of the war but on post-war prospects and policies. A new party had taken the stage, known as Common Wealth. The first by-election was in the King's Lynn constituency in February, where the Conservative majority was reduced from 5,430 to 1,669. The Hon. Somerset Arthur Maxwell, who had represented the constituency since 1935, had died at the age of thirty-seven from wounds received in Middle East fighting. The result was:

Lord Fermoy (Conservative)	10,696
Major F. J. Wise (Independent Socialist)	9,027

In April there was a by-election in the Eddisbury constituency in Cheshire, and two candidates opposed the government's nominee. One of them, Warrant Officer J. Loverseed, representing the Common Wealth party, was an East Anglian, born in Norfolk and educated at the grammar school in Sudbury, which his father had represented in the Commons in 1923–24. Young Loverseed had been a pilot in the Battle of Britain in 1940, and he fought his campaign as an advocate of the Beveridge Report and of nationalisation of land and the coal, electricity, transport and iron and steel industries. The result was:

J. Loverseed (Common Wealth)	8,023
T. Peacock (Liberal National)	7,537
Heathcote Williams (Independent Liberal)	2,803

This was Common Wealth's first election victory. At the Darwen by-election late in the year a journalist, Honor Balfour, standing as an Independent Liberal, polled 8,799 votes and cut the government majority to seventy. There were two recounts. It was another signal that public opinion was resolute. The government created a new post of Minister of Reconstruction, with a seat in the War Cabinet,

Haymaking on Church Farm, Great Glemham, during the summer of 1943. In the background is a B-17 of the 569th Bombardment Squadron at its dispersal on the perimeter of Framlingham airfield.

Mrs Faith Garrard

and appointed one of the most popular and non-partisan of its members to fill it. Lord Woolton, who had been Minister of Food since 1940 and who had gained public confidence to a remarkable degree, now switched his whole attention to post-war reconstruction.

There was a cautionary note in the Christmas Day broadcast to the Empire by King George VI. "While we have bright visions of the future, we have no easy dreams of the days that lie close at hand," he said. The 1943 BBC Christmas programme was entitled "We are advancing, towards victory, towards understanding." As the year ended, the war had lasted longer than the First World War, and no-one could confidently predict how much longer it would go on. Mrs Sarah Williams noted in her diary:

> Sheringham feels the war is nearly at an end, since Lord Woolton has been transferred to the Ministry of Reconstruction. There is definitely much more in the shops this year than last—much poorer quality on the whole, but still plenty.

A couple of days later she noted that "the papers are full of the approaching end of the war". But her anxious private thoughts showed no confidence in a better world ahead:

> For the first time I feel afraid lest Jacob couldn't get a job . . . I saw it said somewhere that we are all suffering from the hangover *before*, instead of after, the celebrations. Certainly people seem depressed.

An East Bergholt housewife wrote to Mass Observation in December:

> I feel that the war in Europe *may* be over in 1944, and that our prospect of ultimate success is no longer in doubt, BUT that we have a very tough job in front of us still, which will require the maximum effort of all concerned. I face this year with the greatest amount of optimism I have experienced so far in this war. I also feel that politically this will be a very critical year. We shall come to grips with social questions so long shelved, and powerful reactionary elements may precipitate a political crisis if the opposing forces are strong enough to stand up for true democratic rights. Immense European problems must also be confronted . . .[4]

A twenty-seven-year-old Chelmsford journalist who was serving in the Royal Corps of Signals offered an equally sober scenario:

> I don't expect the war (nor the war in Europe alone, even) to be over by the end of 1944. It'll be hard slogging all the way to the German border, and not until that's reached is there any chance of a sudden German collapse.[5]

This ambivalence was characteristic of the public mood as 1943 ended. Expectations about the coming Second Front blended eagerness and apprehension. The debate about the world that would follow victory demonstrated idealism and scepticism. One thing was clear; the war had passed its turning point. One day it would end, and in that ending there would be a new beginning. Further effort would be called for to create the better society to which all now aspired. The spirit of William Blake's New Jerusalem had taken hold of the people.

Notes on Sources

Regional newspapers, personal diaries and published biographical accounts of various aspects of the war in East Anglia have been used as principal sources. The *Eastern Daily Press*, the *East Anglian Daily Times* and the *Cambridge Daily News* provided basic coverage of those events which could be freely reported during 1943. Service activity was, of course, subject to censorship, and the sources which have been used are the regimental histories, War Office files at the Public Records Office, and the several authoritative accounts of aerial activity which have been published in recent years. Acknowledgement is made below and references given where appropriate.

Insights into the everyday lives of ordinary civilians who lived in the region are provided by personal diaries held by the Mass Observation Archive at Sussex University, and these have been used extensively. Pseudonyms have been used to conceal actual identities, in order to preserve the confidentiality promised by MO when the diaries were placed in their care, but file references are given.

For the national and international background the standard reference books have been used—the various volumes of the official *History of the Second World War*, published by Her Majesty's Stationery Office, and Sir Winston Churchill's personal account *The Second World War*.

Chapter 1

(1) Robert Arbib: *Here We Are Together*, pages 9–13. Longmans, 1946.
(2) Peter Finch: *Warmen Courageous*—The Story of the Essex Home Guard, pages 169–170. John H. Burrows, 1951.
(3) Roger A. Freeman: *B-17 Fortress at War*. Ian Allen, 1977.
(4) Roger A. Freeman: *The Mighty Eighth*, page 56. Macdonald, 1970.
(5) PRO, Ref. Works 46/7.

Chapter 2

(1) Winston S. Churchill: *The Second World War*, Volume IV, *The Hinge of Fate*, page 609. Cassell, 1951.
(2) Sir Charles Webster and Noble Frankland: *The Strategic Air Offensive against Germany, 1939–45*. Vol 2, page 459. HMSO, 1961.
(3) Ibid., page 5.
(4) Ibid., page 95.
(5) Ibid., page 7.
(6) G. M. Dixon & J. Rippon: *Wings over Eastern England*, Minimax Books, 1980.
(7) Ian Hawkins: *Courage, Honor, Victory,* page 26. 95th Bomb Group (H) Association, 1987.
(8) James Good Brown: *The Mighty Men of the 381st, Heroes All*, page 118. Publishers' Press, Salt Lake City, 1984.
(9) John Comer: *Combat Crew*, page 42. Leo Cooper Ltd, 1988.
(10) James Good Brown, *op. cit.*, page 231.
(11) Ibid., page 215. A detailed and vivid account of the Schweinfurt raid is provided by Cromer, *op. cit.*, pages 122–130.

	National and International	*Regional*
May (continued)	Churchill addresses both Houses of Congress in Washington. All Atlantic U-boats recalled, ending Battle of Atlantic.	Andrews Field opened—first airfield built by US Army Engineers. Chelmsford bombed—Marconi factory disrupted.
June	For first time, no North Atlantic convoy was attacked. French Committee of National Liberation formed. Island of Pantelleria captured. King George VI visits Malta.	Union Society at Cambridge declines to admit women. Derby run at Newmarket. Red Cross organises meetings for families of Japanese POWs.
July	Allied invasion of Sicily. Churchill and Roosevelt issue surrender appeal to Italian people. Rome bombed by USAAF planes. Hitler and Mussolini meet. RAF begin heavy night raids on Hamburg and Ruhr. King Victor Emmanuel III dismisses Mussolini. Marshal Badoglio begins negotiations with Allies.	First postcards received from POWs in Japanese hands. "Farm Sunday"—land girls parade in Cambridge and Ipswich. Regional campaign to collect scrap. West Suffolk turns down proposal for women police. 20,000 at Bury St Edmunds fête for POW Fund.
August	SE Asia Command formed, with Mountbatten as Supreme Commander. Russians resume offensive, capture Orel. Heavy Allied bombing of targets throughout Italy and Germany. Rome declared an open city. US troops take Messina and end Sicily campaign. German troops sent into Italy and the Balkans. Churchill and Roosevelt at Quebec decide to invade Italy in September and confirm "Operation Overlord" with 1.5.44 target date.	Volunteers from towns help on farms. Harvest completed in ideal weather conditions. USAAF lose 91 planes from East Anglian bases in raids on Peenemunde and Schweinfurt. All towns organise "Holidays at Home" programmes.
September	Armistice with Italy signed. Invasion of Italy begins, and 8th Army advances in Calabria. Badoglio announces surrender. Fierce German opposition to US 5th Army landings in Gulf of Salerno.	Invasion troops begin to concentrate in eastern counties. Church and welfare organisations concerned at social problems. Archbishop of Canterbury at Suffolk "Religion and Life" conference.